GW00983889

# GOLF'S
## LIGHTER
### SIDE

# GOLF'S

# LIGHTER

## *SIDE*

Selected from 100 years
of Golf Illustrated

Edited by

## *Chris Plumridge*

*Lennard Publishing*
*1989*

Lennard Publishing
a division of Lennard Books Ltd
Musterlin House, Jordan Hill Road, Oxford OX2 8DP

British Library Cataloguing in Publication Data
Golf's lighter side.
1. Humour in English, 1945– Special subjects:
Golf – Anthologies
I. Plumridge, Chris   II. Golf Illustrated
827′.914′080355

ISBN 1 85291 059 3

First published 1989
© Lennard Books Limited

Editor Michael Leitch
Designed by Cooper-Wilson
Jacket design by Pocknell & Co
Typesetting by Goodfellow & Egan, Cambridge
Printed and bound in Spain by Grupo Nerecan

# CONTENTS

(1891)

## YOUNG AND OLD

(Miles after Kingsley.)
When all the world is young, lad,
Fairway, green and rough,
And every goose a swan, lad,
And no hole seems too tough,
Then hey for your plus-fours, lad,
And round the course away,
The club-house has its bores, lad,
That yammer all the day.
When all the world is old, lad,
And gout affects your pins,
And all the sport is stale, lad,
Compared with copious gins,
The club-house will receive you,
You'll join the would-be wise,
And soon you'll find 'twon't grieve you
To swap appalling lies.

(1927)

# INTRODUCTION

Humour is not usually regarded as a suitable subject for serious analysis. Nonetheless it is an important, not to say vital, part of our lives. Accusing someone of not having a sense of humour is a damning indictment, tantamount to telling a man that he is a lousy driver, a rotten lover and is cruel to animals. (Note: Men always have a sense of humour, women are just good for a laugh.) Even the expression 'a sense of humour' implies that there are several levels of amusement and it is only the connoisseur who can recognise the bouquet of some real vintage stuff.

In truth it's much more basic than that. Humour is perhaps the greatest defence mechanism known to mankind for it is rooted deeply in our instinct for self-preservation. When we see someone slip on a banana skin, we laugh. We laugh because the actual sight of someone falling over has a shock factor which laughter can relieve. But we also laugh because we are delighted the same thing hasn't happened to us. That's the baser instinct.

All of which brings us to golf and the reason you are reading this little opus. To my mind, golf is the ultimate of the banana-skin syndrome. All of us have sniggered inwardly when our opponent has foozled a shot but it's only the unwise or extremely foolish golfer who sniggers without acknowledging that before too long the roles could be reversed.

This mutual sharing of relative ineptitude is what binds us golfers together and gives us the opportunity to develop our sense of humour to that higher plane previously mentioned. Woe betide the man or woman who cannot laugh at himself or herself on the golf course for they are doomed to become lonely and remote figures and may even be forced to turn professional.

Since September 19th, 1890 *Golf Illustrated* has been chronicling the facts, figures and eccentricities of the banana-skin game. As the world's first golf magazine it was a modest affair, comprising just 16 pages and costing twopence. Its style reflected the Victorian age of its birth. This was the era of stout ex-Indian Army Colonels of bellicose manner, of ladies who were unable to take the club back much beyond hip height due to the voluminous clothing they wore, but above all it was the age of the Scots.

The Editor during those early days was quick to latch on to the dour, Calvinistic approach the Celts brought to their second national sport, (drinking still having the edge). Although the humour was much less sophisticated, a swift cartoon depicting an incompetent player and a hairy Scots caddie muttering something unintelligible through his whiskers was always reckoned to be good for a chuckle. The vernacular was frequently used to describe the appeal of the game and there was some excruciating poetry published in the same vein. The Rev. J. Kerr presented this masterpiece for Christmas 1901, the first verse of which gives you some idea of what I mean:

> My blessing' on your sonsie face
> Brave weekly o' the gowffin race
> In every neuk ye've fand a place
> And far and sure
> Nae mortal man can tell your pace
> Ye drive like stoor

Unfortunately this was the standard of humorous writing for the first 40 years of the magazine's existence, which proves once again that the Scots have a great deal to answer for. Much of the editorial in those early days consisted of pages of club results, the publishers believing, and probably quite rightly, that every name printed meant a copy sold to that person. There was also some lively correspondence concerning the issues of the day, one in particular, regarding the correct spelling of 'golf' as against 'gowf' or 'gowff', lasting for weeks.

There were some noble attempts at humorous writing, one or two examples of which are contained within these pages, but it wasn't until the 1930s that a seam of gold was struck. This was a series entitled 'Letters to a Golf Club Secretary' which was originally published in *Punch* and then reproduced in *Golf Illustrated*. More than 50 years later the exploits of General Forecursue, Admiral Sneyring-Stymie, Lionel Nutmeg *et al* and their correspondence with the unfortunate Whelk, Secretary of Roughover GC, still have the authentic ring of genuine self-mocking humour.

Sprinting through the decades, more from necessity than desire, we alight in the period of Tom Scott's editorship which began after World War II and lasted for nearly 30 years. Tom maintained the basics of a weekly

magazine with up-to-the-minute tournament reports, news, readers' correspondence and a modicum of instruction from such as Henry Cotton and
John Jacobs. Tom knew a good thing when he saw one and thus in 1954
took the opportunity to snap up Henry Longhurst as a regular contributor.

Henry was everyone's favourite golf writer, and probably still is more
than ten years after his death. He was not a humorous writer in the style of a
Wodehouse but he covered the moments of the day with a light, deft touch
and, like Wodehouse, kept it simple. For 15 years Henry amused and
entertained the magazine's readers and no compilation such as this would be
complete without his contribution.

In more recent years humour in golf has taken on a far more irreverent
tone. Sacred cows have been slaughtered by the writers' and cartoonists'
art. Practically every part of the game has been given the treatment with
people such as Peter Dobereiner and Michael McDonnell, and even a
fellow called Plumridge, bringing a touch of mirth into the serious business
of getting the ball into the hole in the fewest number of strokes.

One of the drawbacks of putting together a collection such as this is that
progress can be interminably slow. This is simply because the sheer volume
of fascinating facts and information is such that it is easy to become
involved in, say, the 1894 Open Championship report or Harold Hilton's
thoughts on the backswing or a complete swing sequence of Bobby Jones.
The price of a golf ball in 1902, the creation of new and marvellous aids to
improve the swing, the changing fashions, the implementation of the
Rules, the development of equipment – all and much more are contained
within a century of covering the game.

This book is an attempt to reveal the lighter side of golf through those
100 years. I am sure that every golfer will find something within its pages
which will raise a smile, if not a belly-laugh. If it achieves nothing else, it
will serve as a reminder that the opportunity for a good laugh is never far
from the surface whenever a golf ball is being struck. Remember that the
next time you go out to play. Oh yes, and look out for the banana-skin.

Chris Plumridge

# CLUB LIFE

## Midwinter Madness

*Peter Dobereiner*

At the risk of adding ammunition to the anti-golf brigade who claim that all golfers are anti-social, selfish, snobbish and emotionally unstable, I must admit that at this time of year a certain element of skittishness seems to possess normally staid golfers.

When the frost is on the ground and the greens have been declared out of bounds in the interests of preserving the sacred turf, a form of midwinter madness infects the membership.

Sober rural deans come into the bar and cry: "Anybody for a gang bang?" During one particularly cold snap some years ago I actually heard a bank manager shout: "Who wants a drink?" Stern faced scratchmen, who are normally only to be seen in the club nodding condescendingly to committee chairmen as they pick up their clubs for a county match, suddenly become almost human and roguishly declare: "What a day for a spot of hockey knockers."

There are, I suspect, several contributory reasons why golfers begin to thaw when the temperature drops below zero. Firstly, there is the normal euphoria of the festive season. The alcoholic fumes tend to hang about in the atmosphere and pervade every corner of the club.

I have heard it said that at one club, with a high proportion of Scots membership, a pair of the captain's old socks which had lain on top of his locker for years, was tested at 90-proof five weeks after the New Year's Eve party.

Then there is the Christmas present syndrome. Keen golfers with non-golfing relations tend to be given all manner of novelties of a supposedly humorous nature. They all come out at this time of year. Putters with heads in the shape of bananas, funny head covers and, yes, crutch hooks. This last item is a kind of sling with a forehead strap and a . . . well, it is supposed to make you keep your head down and I am sure you can imagine the rest.

## FRIVOLOUS VARIANTS

They are all good for a ribald giggle in the bar. But I believe that the main reason for winter madness is simply the fact that we are on temporary greens. That means that serious golf is out. _Ergo_, what golf there is to be played must be of a non-serious, or frivolous nature.

There is also the fact that it is so cold that nobody wants to hang about lining up putts. You haven't a hope of holing out over the corrugated-iron surface of the temporary green, anyway, so why linger? You take a quick stab, curse your luck and march on. The nett effect of all these factors is that the games golfers play at this time of the year are curious variations which give the addict his regular fix but at the same time return him to the comfort of the bar in the shortest possible order.

Now comes a curious point. The most entertaining versions of winter golf are always played at somebody else's golf club. In my golfing circle we sometimes play chairman when there are only three participants. (You become chairman by winning a hole outright from the other two, and collect the money if you then, while in the chair, win a hole.)

We also split six points among three. (All half – two points each; if A beats B who beats C, split 4, 2, 0; if A beats B and C who half, split 4, 1, 1.) Personally I can never keep track of the points situation in this method.

Then there is the standard gang bang in which any number of competitors can play although seven is about the upper limit in the interests of fast play, even with players picking up their balls once they are out of a hole. This is simply a case of getting a point if you win a hole outright from all the others and very difficult it is to gather points.

None of these forms is in the slightest degree original, which brings me back to my point about other people's golf clubs. Occasionally someone introduces a visitor who joins us for a convivial round of chairman. Then, when he has duly trousered the kitty and we are back in the club among the tea and toast, he remarks: "Well, that was most agreeable. You know, back at my club we have this fantastic game in the winter where you all pick a different golf club. What you do is . . . it really is hilarious . . . well, there is this bottle of whisky. By the way, did I mention that you choose teams before you go out? That's a riot in itself because we have this character who plays the northern clubs, a fabulous comedian who is a genuinely funny man, none of your Pagliacci stuff, all serious when he isn't on stage. Anyway, where was I? . . ."

FORE!

(1897)

The answer to that question is, of course, that the listener is in a state of total confusion. All he has gathered is that it is a good game, whatever it is. Even if the visitor can be persuaded to explain in logical sequence and full detail, nobody can remember how it went afterwards. That is almost a law of nature, that no game can proceed smoothly simply on the basis of verbal instructions beforehand. You have to go out and do it before you get the hang of any game and, of course, that could only happen if the visiting expert returned. Which he does not. (I defy any man or woman who has never played badminton to master the intricacies of who serves to whom and from where and when in doubles from simply reading the rules. Play it a dozen times or so and the system gradually begins to sink in.)

So what I suggest is this. In the interests of spreading happiness throughout the land in these bleak times could we please appeal for details of novel and proven varieties of winter golf. I am sure the Editor of *Golf Illustrated* will be more than happy to publish original ideas.

Does the twelve-inch hole really work in practice on temporary greens? Does anybody play to an old oil drum instead of a hole? How do those matches work out with each player carrying a different club?

Let's be hearing from you with all those local variations of winter golf. Who knows, it could start a new rage. At worst it will help to get us through this damned awful weather.

(1974)

## Unaccustomed as I am to Public Speaking
*Chris Plumridge*

It is now the season of the golf club dinner and all over the country club captains and various other dignitaries are standing in front of bathroom mirrors mouthing the words "Unaccustomed as I am to public speaking". This, of course, is the chief problem about many after-dinner speakers, they *are* unaccustomed to public speaking and it is only after the audience has sat through 45 minutes of some turgid litany on the state of the greens, the refurbishment of the locker-room plus the recounting of some dreadfully old golfing joke that the listeners realise just how unaccustomed they are.

There are certain ground rules regarding after-dinner speaking, the most important of which is "Keep it brief". Five minutes of straight-down-the-middle stuff will endear you far more to your audience than 25 minutes rambling through the rough of your golfing memories. Another golden rule is never preface a joke with the words "Which reminds me of a story . . ." To begin with, this remark warns the audience that you are about to tell a joke which they have, in all probability, heard before and secondly, even if they haven't heard it before, that introductory remark will certainly guarantee a lukewarm response. It is far better to work your golfing stories into the text of your speech so that they arrive unexpectedly, but, by and large, unless you are an accomplished and well-practised speaker, it is best to avoid the "funnies".

Of all the golfing speeches that I have heard, and by God I've heard a few, only three stand out. They were delivered by Henry Longhurst, Bill (Lord) Deedes and a former President of the English Golf Union, John Wild. The first two were both journalists and had led such interesting and varied lives that one could have listened to them long after the last decanter of port had passed by. John Wild is not a journalist but his recounting, delivered in flat Lancashire tones, of how he tried to persuade the R & A to stage the Open Championship at his home club in Wigan is well worth catching if you have the opportunity.

### WORLD BORES XI

For the golf correspondent attending a dinner, not as a speaker but as a guest, there are two pitfalls – being bored before dinner and being bored during dinner.

Before dinner there is always the likelihood that you will be trapped in a corner by somebody who wishes to tell you what he thinks about the Ryder Cup/the Open Championship/Severiano Ballesteros and how he never reads your stuff anyway. The best way to combat this individual is firstly to arm yourself with two drinks. This enables you to interrupt his flow by saying "I'd love to listen to you but I really must take this drink over to my friend". The late Pat Ward-Thomas of *The Guardian* had a word for those sort of people – he called them "Pinners" and I believe it was he and Gerald Micklem who once sat down to compile a World Bores XI with selection being made from those people they had met through golf. I cannot reveal the full team line-up since many of them are still around but I can tell you that the opening pair were a Scotsman and an Australian who could be guaranteed to take the shine off any new ball.

Being bored during dinner is another matter altogether since there is usually no escape. If you find yourself in this position you may care to adopt a system I devised while I was at school and forced, every Sunday, to sit through the mandatory sermon by various visiting ecclesiastical bores.

The system worked on the basis of every time the Lord's name was mentioned it indicated a shot of true class and when the forces of darkness and evil were invoked, a shot that was not so good. Thus, if the visiting churchman chose for his text: "And the Lord said, get thee behind me Satan" you were off the first with a good drive but missed the green with the second. A course was selected according to the parish from which the priest came and on this basis I once went round Little Aston with the then Bishop of Birmingham, a very devout man, in 52. I hasten to add that a particularly fiery Ulster clergyman once cost me a 98 at Royal County Down.

This system can be applied to after-dinner speeches using certain well-worn clichés for scoring. For example, "At the risk of boring you" could be regarded as a definite birdie chance, and if followed by "but I must tell you this little story about the chap who sliced off the first and the ball hit the driver of a bus which then ran into a shop . . . " then you can claim you holed the putt. Incidentally, that particular story, which I'm sure you've heard, ends with a policeman going up to a golfer and asking him what he's to do about all the damage, to which the golfer replies "Well, I'm thinking of moving my right hand a little more under the shaft".

The reason for repeating it is that something very similar recently occurred in quite spectacular fashion in the West African state of Benin. It appears that a factory overseer, Mathieu Boya, was practising during his lunch break next to the country's main air base. One of his shots sliced the ball over the fence where it hit a bird. The bird then plummeted through the windscreen of a jet that was about to take off. The pilot wrestled with the controls but was unable to prevent his aircraft from crashing into four other jets parked on the runway, thereby destroying the country's entire air force. The police then confronted the luckless Mr Boya, presented him with a bill for £26 million and asked him what he was going to do about it. So far, Mr Boya's reply is not on record since he is currently languishing in jail charged with "hooliganism" but you know what I would have said, don't you?

(1987)

## "Like, I'm not in the Disco Scene, Man!"

*Peter Dobereiner*

I must congratulate the secretary of Basingstoke golf club on his perspicacity. In *Golf Illustrated* of April 18th commented on a recent article of mine and drew a vivid picture of how he saw the author in his imagination. "O Wad some Pow'r the giftie gie us, To see oursels as others see us," wrote Rabbie Burns and now, praise be, some power has done exactly that in my case.

"One single person who combines all the sins and omissions of present day young golfers" . . . "an expensively but tastelessly dressed young man" . . . "wearing golf shoes leaning over the bar talking on Christian name matey terms with some long suffering steward" . . . "he has just come off the course, not changing his clothes of course" . . . "not having replaced a single (large) divot" . . . "having dropped the flagstick heavily on every green" . . . "having missed a number of short putts" . . . "is loud in his condemnation of the Greens Committee" . . . "desires a hell on earth golf club with deafening disco music" . . . "grumbling, but ask him to take on a job to help the club and you can't see him for dust".

The secretary scores a number of direct hits, but perhaps I may be permitted to take his points one by one.

**One single person etc:** The wife had a good old chuckle with my probation officer over this bit and they felt it was about right. I thought it a bit steep. Taking the Old Testament view of sin, there are a couple of Commandments I haven't even attempted to break. On the other hand, on the more modest seven-sin scale of Dr Johann Faustus which so absorbed Christopher Marlowe and Goethe, I suppose there is no point in trying to deny my pride, covetousness, wrath, envy, gluttony, sloth and lust.

**Expensive but tasteless dress:** Oh, come on! Only the other week I finally had to face the fact that either I must replace my demob suit or risk arrest. In the bargain basement of the cheapest department store in Augusta, Georgia, I selected an (admittedly tasteless) jacket and engaged the sales-woman in negotiations. She said: "Ah jerst lurve ta heah you-all towalk." "In that case," said I, "let us talk some more and haggle over the price". She trilled with laughter and said: "Have you-all seen the ticket; this heah has been marked down fav tayums olriddy." The price was four dollars, 75 cents, or just over a couple of quid.

**Matey talk with steward:** It is true that during Christmas week I did

THE MAN WHO ARRIVED AT THE COUNTRY CLUB WITH A MIXED BAG

Don't make an unforgivable faux pas—match up with

*Players who prefer a greater amount of whip in their shafts can now obtain the* **TRUE TEMPER LIMBERSHAFT.** *The* **TWIN TAPER** *type of shaft and also the* **HEYES** *Cushion Grip are now obtainable in* **TRUE TEMPER** *woods and* **TRUE TEMPER** *Master Irons*

# TRUE TEMPER STEEL SHAFTS

*All True Temper Shafts are made in a large variety of attractive finishes, Chromium, Black, light and dark grained enamel, light and dark sheath. Your Pro. will gladly let you try them.*

*Made for* British Steel Golf Shafts Ltd., *of 26, Exchange Street East, Liverpool, by Accles & Pollock, Ltd., of Oldbury, Birmingham.*

(1934)

remark to the steward: "Same again all round, please Charlie." There is a widespread feeling within the club that I do not engage in this form of social contact with the bar staff often enough.

**Not changing clothes after play:** Bang on. See above remarks on snappy dressing.

**Large divots:** I consider the size of a man's divots to be an intensely personal matter and not a fit subject for public debate.

**Dropping flagstick on green:** Wide of the mark, alas. My golf consists almost exclusively of four-ball play. My role in the proceedings normally consists of pocketing my ball after taking four hacks at the thing in a bunker and saying to my partner: "I'm afraid this hole is up to you, cock" and walking directly to the next tee. Would that I had the chance to drop the flagstick more often.

**Missing short putts:** You have been spying on me.

**And loudly complaining about the greens committee:** That proves you must have been spying.

**Desires disco music hell:** Like I am not into the disco scene, man. I don't dig even such an inoffensive trio as Olivia, Newt and John. Pop-music, in short, I find decidedly un-heavy, trip-wise. My musical bag is strictly squaresville. For me, Freddy Chopin is out of sight; the modern's best out of earshot.

**Grumbling and running for cover when asked to help:** This is rather a sore point. The inference that I could make a valuable contribution to the deliberations of the various committees is well made. With my distin-guished background in agronomy, catering, management and a lifelong study of the liquor trade (a real labour of love in this last case, my researches frequently leaving me exhausted and red-eyed the following morning) I would be a perfect selection for any committee. By some extraordinary aberration of the democratic processes, I never seem to get nominated, much less elected. However, there is always the possibility of being co-opted and one drops hints in subtle little ways. The other day I kissed the hem of the captain's rain-jacket and all he did was rebuke me for ruining the water-proofing. The chairman of the house committee has let it be known that he does not care to have me lick the polish off his spiked shoes. Short of making a formal complaint to the Race Relations Board on the grounds of discrimination – there is no representation on any of our committees by a member with Black Foot Indian origins – I cannot see what more I can do. Lord knows I am willing, but whenever I broach the subject you cannot see the committees for dust. Well, it is their loss. Just because I am away for ten months in the year is no reason for not asking me, is it? I'll bet Basingstoke golf club would have me on all the committees.

But I do not complain. I am not one to kick against the pricks – except that I do wish that when I write an article seeking to guarantee a supply of trained and dedicated stewards and greenkeepers for this great game that those who disagree with me would stick more or less to the point

However, Mr Secretary, as one who was almost (accidentally) shot in the prohibition gang warfare of New York and whose sixpence pocket money used to purchase half a pint of beer, five Woodbines and a packet of crisps, I forgive you everything for those constantly repeated references to my youth.

(1974)

## Letters from the Steward

Sodsbury Golf Club
Sodsbury
Divotshire
1AM 4UP

Sir,

Firstly, I must thank you most sincerely for deciding to publish my letter. Gretel was thrilled and says that any time you fancy a culinary ménage à deux, she'd love to prepare a few of her delicacies for you.

You will have noticed I am sure, that I have so far made no mention of the actual game of golf. Well, there are two reasons for this. Firstly, your magazine is already full of erudite comment, and secondly, I don't know anything about the game. I have been told by those in the know that it's a great stress reliever. If this is true, then the human body is a great deal cleverer than I ever thought it was. It must be able to differentiate quite clearly between the agonies of declining sales figures and the physical and mental trauma brought about by trying to break a tungsten shafted putter over your right knee.

Anyway, to change the subject completely – aren't golf club Secretaries a funny breed? Ours is a nice enough old boy really – Old Etonian and ex-RAF (He failed Sandhurst) and he lisps his r's. So he calls us "Gwetel and Scwoggins". Actually, I think he's got a bit of a soft spot for Gretel, but then, so he has for most of the ladies in the club. He's never married but as far as I know, he's quite "normal". Certainly, the silly smile on Evadne Flappit's face the other evening suggests that he is. I mean really, who's going to believe that it takes over an hour to pay a subscription? Mind you, Evadne doesn't have a lot to smile about – unless you think a moustache is funny.

And then of course, there are the Committees – and what a motley crew they are. I swear that they are the originators of that famous saying, "The decision is maybe, and that's final!" And the rivalry that exists between them is unbelievable.

The House Committee refuse to discuss the kitchen alterations with the Catering Committee, and neither of them discuss anything with us. But they are all experts of course, never mind that their expertise is in such diverse areas as dentistry, scrap metal dealing, *et al.* Frankly, they mostly strike me as a collection of tired executives living out their business fantasies in an unquestioning world.

Mind you, as someone once said, "No matter how you slice it, it's still salami."

Yours sincerely,
Norman F. Scroggins
Steward

(1986)

———————————

Sodsbury Golf Club
Sodsbury
Divotshire
1AM 4UP

Sir,

Firstly, I must thank you most sincerely for the cheque. When I wrote to you originally, I was certainly not expecting to be paid, so that was a pleasant surprise. Just one thing though – my bank manager says that if you signed it as well, I could pay it in rather than keep it as a souvenir. Funny chaps bank managers – no sense of occasion.

Meanwhile, back at Sodsbury, the Committee have been at it again. They had their monthly séance last night, when they all sit around the table holding hands trying to make contact with the living. This time, they had a major issue to resolve which had been passed to them by the Ladies' Section. Was it really true, the ladies wanted to know, that a pot of tea for one was going up from 17p to 20p, and if so did the Committee find this acceptable?

Now, the Committee, of course, are not world famous for their consumption of tea, whereas the Ladies all have honours degrees in the pricing of anything non-alcoholic, led by the formidable Mrs Gobblethrust, of salmon and cucumber sandwich fame. The Captain immediately suggested that the situation was serious enough to be referred to both the Chairman of House and the Chairman of Finance and that they should be invited to report back to the next full meeting. Since this was certainly one of the Captain's braver and more incisive decisions, it attracted considerable support until Ivor Fairshot, Chairman of Greens and never one to be outwitted by the ladies, came up with the answer. The Ladies were to be told that due to declining catering profits, the £1,250 budgeted for the re-decoration of the ladies' changing room was reluctantly being reduced to £1,000 – unless of course the ladies had, with their expert knowledge, any suggestions . . .? Round the bar afterwards, words like 'brilliant' and 'fantastic' were much used, and there is little doubt that Ivor Fairshot's chance of being the next Vice-Captain has become a virtual certainty. Mind you, he must be careful not to solve too many problems in case people become nervous!

I wouldn't like you to think by the way, that I've got an exaggeratedly low opinion of committees, but let's put it this way – if Hitler had been a committee, I should think that the second world war would be starting about now.

Anyway, enough's enough – I'll write again soon.

Yours faithfully,
Norman F. Scroggins
Steward

Sodsbury Golf Club
Sodsbury
Divotshire
1AM 4UP

Sir,

Well, here we are in the season of Big Events at Sodsbury. The Divotshire Mixed Knockout went very well except that once again the Secretary displayed his total inability to work out a draw sheet. Apparently, when he was sports officer of his RAF base, if there weren't exactly sixteen, thirty-two, etc., entrants for an event, he would detail people off to make up the numbers so that there were no byes involved. Here, of course, that's not possible, so what he does is to write in fictitious names to round up the entry. He then tells the members involved that the imaginary opponent has conceded a walkover. This system normally works, but due to a succession of people scratching, business trips, summer flu, etc., the Captain ended up in the semi-finals with three non-existent members! He was only mollified by the fact that he's never before had his name on a club Honours board and the Secretary's promise not to allow overseas members to enter in future!

I must admit that the event that Gretel and I like least is when a member uses the Club as the venue for his Annual Works Outing. We had one yesterday and it was typical of such occasions. John Boot, of garage chain fame, is an insignificant but pleasant enough chap, but his wife is a totally different matter. She strode through the door like a ship of the line under full sail, all taffeta and Rive Gauche, and "took over". Her stentorian tones could be heard all over the clubhouse, and I really felt for poor "Bootsy" as she called him. The last straw was when the last three out, having been told they were playing a three ball and never having played before, took five and a quarter hours to go round – playing three balls each!

Finally, Sir, I must protest. I mean, I know you pundits at *Golf Illustrated* pride yourselves on being "First with the News", but when I opened your last issue and found that my job was being advertised, I thought that it was taking things a bit far. Hopefully, it's all a misunderstanding and I can sort it out. If so, I'll write again soon.

Yours faithfully,
Norman F. Scroggins
Steward

(1986)

Sodsbury Golf Club
Sodsbury
Divotshire
1AM 4UP

Sir,

What excitement we've had at Sodsbury these last few days! You see, once every three months a select group from the Committee interview potential new members, and a week ago Friday was the last time. Well, apparently this chap had 'phoned up and had a long chat with the Secretary who was most impressed. So, one application form and ten days later, in he walks for interview – immaculately dressed, Gucci shoes and tie, beautifully spoken, and black as a pint of draught Guinness!

You can imagine the confusion. I have never before seen any of our Committee falling over themselves to be so polite, so friendly, so generous, but above all – so unbiased. And when Ivor Fairshot, Chairman of Greens, walked in and the applicant was introduced as Jonathan Whiteman, I honestly thought he was going to have an apoplectic fit.

Anyway, the interview went ahead, and needless to say I was somewhat over-solicitous in my endeavours to make sure that they had all the drinks they wanted. Some of the remarks I overheard were almost too good to be true.

Ivor Fairshot: ". . . now in this club, we've always believed in calling a spade a spade and er, well yes."

The Captain: "Er, I think it's only fair to tell you, Mr, er, Whiteman, that this is an extremely difficult course." Left hanging hopefully.

The Applicant: "Well, I must admit that in the last few months my handicap has crept up to 4.8 but if I could get a few rounds in, it will probably come down again – it usually does." Silence.

Then, finally, I had one of those opportunities, the like of which only occurs once in a lifetime. Into the bar came a liveried chauffeur who asked me if I could get a message to His Serene Highness that he was in danger of being late for his dinner at the Mansion House. Couldn't I just!

I wrote the message on a piece of paper and quietly put it down in front of the Captain. The confusion was spectacular! Apologies from the applicant who explained that he never used his title in his private life. Much clicking of the heels from the Secretary who would have put his Wing Commander's uniform on if he'd had time, and "Good night, your Sereneship" from Ivor who was never much use at protocol.

I think he'll get in, but I'll let you know.

Yours faithfully,
Norman F. Scroggins
Steward

(1986)

(1891)

## Letters to the Secretary of a Golf Club

*G.C. Nash*

### THE CLUB MUSEUM

[*From Mrs Wobblegoose (Stewardess, Roughover Golf Club)*]
Dear Sir, I have been hearing from the Steward all about the Museum and Sir I felt that you would be interested to have the chopbone on which Admiral Sneyring-Stymie's brother-in-law broke his eye-tooth in 1939.

It has always been one of my treasured possessions, but if you would like it I should be most welcome to give it up.

Yours faithfully,
Lottie Wobblegoose

[_From Barnabas Hackett (Member of Roughover Golf Club)_]
Dear Sir, I do hope you will not mind my writing and suggesting that the Club should start a museum. After all, time is jogging on, and, although many of us remember the early days of golf only too well, generations to come would, I am sure, be interested in such relics as old clubs, gutty balls, etc.

As I feel sure my suggestion will appeal to you, I am sending herewith one of the original socket-headed drivers.

Yours faithfully,
B. Hackett

PS. I would suggest that the big glass case in the Reading Room be used for this purpose and the cups at present there be transferred to the long top-shelf in the Bar.
PS. 2. Why not circularise members about it? I am sure there must be quite a few who could send you something.

---

[_From Lionel Nutmeg, Malayan Civil Service (Rtd.), Old Bucks Cottage, Roughover_]
Dear Sir, I enclose some hairs from the Aberdeen Angus bull which I hit with my drive at the second hole on May 1st, 1938. I discovered them adhering to my ball and I have kept them in the back of my watchcover every since.

As a matter of historic interest, I may say that for a time they brought me the most amazing good fortune, but for the last four years they have been worse than useless.

I suggest that in showing them you have them tied up with a small piece of blue ribbon and laid out on white satin in a black pill-box.

Yours faithfully,
L. Nutmeg

PS. I am leaving to the Club in my will the cornet which I played at the last Annual Dinner.

[*From Rupert Bindweed, Fig Tree Villa, Roughover*]
Dear Sir, I enclose for the Museum the sketch of a coat-of-arms which my brother blazoned for the Club in 1925. It comprises: "Argent on a fess of gules between three rabbits at gaze vert, as many golf-balls argent"; or at least that's what I think he told me it was.

The committee at that time were an extremely ignorant set of men, and they turned it down.

Yours faithfully,
R. Bindweed

---

[*From John Baggs (Caddiemaster, Roughover)*]
Mr Whelk, Sir, Hearing about the Museum I enclose herewith the autograph of the late House-Steward that went off with the case of liqueur brandy and afterwards got jailed for stealing the Town Clerk's ring.

Although Jos. Stewart was a Club Servant I never got my one and six.

Yours sir,
John Baggs

---

[*From Admiral Charles Sneyring-Stymie, C.B., The Bents, Roughover*]
Dear Sir, I am sending by Special Messenger for the Museum the stuffed trout which I killed with my second at the fifth (stream hole) in 1933.

You may have heard that there was some difference of opinion at the time as to whether it was my trophy or not, some maintaining that it had been killed by an otter, others that it had died of old age.

The fact, however, remains that when I came upon the fish it was lying in shallow water with my golf-ball close beside it. To me the evidence was quite conclusive and I felt more than justified in having it mounted.

Yours faithfully,
Charles Sneyring-Stymie

---

[*From Doctor Edwin Sockett, Medical Practitioner, Roughover*]
*Club Museum*
Dear Whelk, In reply to your circular I enclose herewith the score card pencil I extracted from George Humpitt's abdomen last June.

I am also sending along the salmon-gaff with which General Sir Armstrong Forcursue won the fourth hole in his match with Prince Suva Ibrahim bin Mackintosh Abdulla on 10-7-54. Please find as well the stuffed mongoose which the latter left on my hall-table by way of a fee when I patched him up.

Yours sincerely,
E. Sockett

---

[*From General Sir Armstrong Forcursue, K.B.E., C.S.I. (captain, Roughover Golf Club)*]
Sir, The smell in the Reading Room since you started that damned Museum in intolerable. This morning I had to read my paper in the Locker Room. Unless you do something about this immediately there will be trouble.

Yours faithfully,
Armstrong Forcursue

---

[*From Ephraim Wobblegoose (House Steward, Roughover Golf Club)*]
Dear Sir, I have tried moth-balls, disinfectant sprays and even the new floor-polish which the traveller said would rout the beetles, but Sir it was all no good, so I did as you bid and burnt everything.

Hope the chill is mending and you will be back soon.

Yours Sir,
E. Wobblegoose

## FIXING MATCHES

[*From Admiral Charles Sneyring-Stymie, C.B., The Bents, Roughover*]
Sir, Why did you persuade me to go and play golf with that visitor this morning? I discovered before we had left the 3rd tee that he was an insurance agent, and before I had holed out at the 4th he was trying to sell my golfer's public liability policy.

Granted I hit him on the foot when driving at the 2nd, but even so I consider his opportunism in very bad taste, and I would have you know that if you arrange matches like this for me again you can look out for trouble.

Your faithfully,
Charles Sneyring-Stymie

[*From General Sir Armstrong Forcursue, K.B.E., C.S.I., "The Cedars",
Roughover*]
Dear Sir, Why can you never find decent people for me to play with? This
week has been a fair example of many others, and I feel it only right to let
you know what I have had to put up with. Here, then, is a résumé of my
opponents:

(a)  Monday. A poet wearing a red and white check cap, who waggled his
club at least 35 times before each shot.

(b)  Tuesday. A retired major in the Australian Army, who did nothing
but talk about kangaroos and how the Tibetans dispose of their dead.

(c)  Wednesday. A parson with a patent peg tee, which whistled until
picked up and switched off.

(d)  Thursday. A vegetarian who once stayed under water for over four
minutes. (Not long enough!)

(e)  Friday. A French count who took 5s. off me by blowing his nose like
a trumpeting elephant whenever I was about to putt.

(f)  This morning. A youth who smelt over-poweringly of hair oil.

(g)  This afternoon (nine holes). A retired sea captain who bounced up
and down when addressing his ball and before every shot shouted out:
"One, two, three – poop!"

Unless you can do better than this there will be trouble.

Yours faithfully,
Armstrong Forcursue

PS. The only thing to be said in favour of the above people is that I would
sooner play with them than with Sneyring-Stymie, Nettle or Nutmeg.

---

[*From Lionel Nutmeg, Malayan Civil Service (Retd.), Old Bucks Cottage,
Roughover*]
My Dear Mr Whelk, I am afraid I do not often write you a complimentary
letter, but I feel it only just that you should know how very much I enjoyed
my game today with Mr Elijah Knuckle.

Mr K is one of the most charming men I have ever met, and he really did
seem so interested to hear all about my long and arduous service in Malaya.

Might I also add that I thought the course never played better – a big
factor in my great victory of 8 and 7.

Yours very sincerely,
Lionel Nutmeg

[_From Barnabus Hackett, Roughover_]
Dear Sir, I wish to complain about the visitor you asked me to give a game to yesterday; and may I say that I have rarely had a more unpleasant round.

Whether it was his boots, or something in his bag, or his braces, I was unable to discover, but the fact remains that during the entire 18 holes he never once stopped creaking. The noise gradually got on my nerves to such an extent that I eventually lost my match.

He wanted me to play again on Thursday, but you can tell him there is nothing doing unless he has the trouble remedied.

Yours faithfully,
B. Hackett

---

[_From Commander Harrington Nettle, C.M.G., D.S.O., Flagstaff Villa, Roughover_]
Sir, On Tuesday you fixed me up for a game of golf with a Mr. Kroup, telling me that the man was very deaf and that I must speak up; but after he had beaten me on the 15th green and I had eased my feelings by saying (in a subdued voice) just what I thought of him, I was much put out when he immediately rounded on me and blurted out that I was a "dirty cad" too.

On making enquiries from his caddie I found out that Mr Kroup is not deaf at all, but that it is his brother who is thus afflicted.

Kindly inform me your reason for being such a fool.

Yours faithfully,
Harrington Nettle

---

[_From Angus McWhigg, Glenfag, Roughover_]
Dear Sir, The man I played golf with this morning, a Mr Jacob Sprogg, went off without paying the stakes for which we agreed to play. The sum amounted to 1s. 3d. (1s. on the match and 3d. on the bye).

As you introduced me to Mr. S kindly note that I hold you responsible for the collection of the debt. Please therefore remit stamps or postal order at your earliest convenience.

Yours faithfully,
Angus McWhigg

[*From Rupert Bindweed, Fig Tree Villa, Roughover*]
Dear Sir, May I suggest that in future when you introduce one golfer to another you do so in an orthodox manner?

You will remember that yesterday you produced an opponent for me and told me that he was tight.

Acting on this information (given as I thought by one sportsman to another) I backed myself for 10s.

It was not, however, until the 3rd hole that I discovered his name was Tyte and that he was as sober as a judge.

Had you introduced him as Mr Tyte I should not have been placed in such a false position.

In the meantime I shall not report this unfortunate incident to the committee – but only on the condition that you put the matter right with me at the 19th hole at an early date.

Yours faithfully,
Rupert Bindweed


## ETIQUETTE

[*From General Sir Armstrong Forcursue, K.B.E., C.S.I. (Captain, Roughover Golf Club)*]
Sir, The Etiquette amongst members is getting worse and worse, so will you please put up several very large notices in different parts of the club on which are printed in red or purple the ten approved rules.

I shall also be glad if you will conceal yourself about the links for the next few days and report all transgressors to me.

Yours faithfully,
Armstrong Forcursue

PS. Kindly post (registered) a copy of the Rules of Etiquette to Lionel Nutmeg. He had lost his ball at the 16th this morning and quite gave me the impression (until I spoke harshly to him) that he was disinclined to let me go through.

*[From Ignatius Thudd, Roughover]*

Dear Sir, I think it is in very bad taste your putting up those notices on etiquette, you might think that members did not know how to behave, and I presume the next thing that we may expect are a set of regulations for the dining-room regarding the eating of soup, asparagus, etc. It is a great pity you do not attend to manners of the club staff and practise what you preach, as I overheard the waitress talking about a napkin as a serviette the other day.

Yours faithfully,
I. Thudd

PS. I wish to report General Forcursue for not replacing his divots at the 2nd, 5th, 6th, 7th, 8th, 9th, 10th, 11th, 13th (three very big ones), 14th, 15th, 16th, 17th, and 18th holes.

*[From General Sir Armstrong Forcursue, K.B.E., C.S.I. (captain, Roughover Golf Club)]*

Sir, I am in receipt of yours of the 23rd enclosing copies of letters sent to you by all those nincompoops, but I should have thought that even they would have known it was a widely recognised fact that all captains of golf clubs are privileged persons. However, as they do not seem to appreciate this, I shall be glad if you will make the matter known to them at your earliest convenience.

   With regard to your personal report on what you call my "delinquencies," I am coming to see you about this at 10 am sharp tomorrow. If you are not in there will be trouble.

Yours faithfully,
Armstrong Forcursue

PS. Why is it that whenever I try and do anything for the benefit of the club I am always misunderstood.
PS.2 You have no tact. As secretary, and knowing the members as you do, it was up to you to have foreseen what has now occurred and argued me out of insisting the notices be put up.
PS.3 Take down the notices immediately.

[*From Herbert Pinhigh, J.P., Roughover*]
Dear Sir, One of the Rules of Etiquette reads, "no one should move or talk or stand close to or directly behind the ball or the hole when a player is making a stroke."

I beg to draw you attention to the fact that General Forcursue shuffled his feet and talked incessantly about "nervous strain when putting for the match" as I was holing out for a half with him on the 18th green this morning – not only that, but also for saying out loud, after the ball went into the tin, that it was fluke and I was no gentleman.

Who is the president or patron of the club? – I should like to bring the captain's disgraceful behaviour to the notice of someone who has a little authority.

Yours faithfully,
Herbert Pinhigh

[*From Ezekiel Higgs, Links Road, Roughover*]
Sir, As you know, it is the unwritten law at Roughover Golf Club that when handicaps are equal it is the older player who has the honour on the first tee.

When General Forcursue and I went out to play yesterday I discovered that our handicaps are both 22, whilst our age is also the same, my birthday being on the June 1st.

After I had tendered him this latter information he immediately pointed out that his birthday was on May 31st, but naturally I was not going to accept his word for such a blatant and unconvincing rejoinder, so that with his failure to produce a birth certificate I cancelled the game.

You should have a list of the certified ages of members stuck up on the first tee so that this sort of thing may not occur.

Yours faithfully,
Ezekiel Higgs

---

[*From Admiral Sneyring-Stymie, C.B., The Bents, Roughover*]
Sir, I regret to inform you that the captain is not only sadly lacking in etiquette but that he is also a liar.

This morning at the 10th he laid me what I claimed as a very definite stymie. I asked him to remove his ball which he refused to do, as he said he still played stymies.

I would not have reported him had he not guffawed loudly when I inadvertently knocked his ball into the hole.

Yours faithfully,
C. Sneyring-Stymie

PS. Your own etiquette leaves much to be desired; why did you not stand up when I came into your office this morning to complain about the lack of heat given out by the Reading Room fire?

---

[*From Tom Bunkerly, MP, Sandy Neuk, Roughover*]
Dear Sir, General Forcursue landed in the bunker at the 9th this morning and took 31 to get out.

I happened to be playing just behind him and also put my ball in the same bunker, and really you might have thought a mad bull had spent the night there.

As General Forcursue is the captain of the club I should be glad if you will ask him to set a better example to his fellow members and to tidy up all hazards, etc., when he has finished using them.

Yours truly,
Tom Bunkerly

# ROOM FOR IMPROVEMENT

## Holes-In-One

*Henry Longhurst*

Now I come to think of it, I can only remember once having seen a hole done in one. This was at the 14th at Alwoodley by an old friend, Mr Brian Ambler, and it was a perfect shot in fact as well as in theory, straight through a strong left-hand wind, never leaving the flag. A few months later I received a wire from him saying simply "Done it again."

It was a former secretary of Alwoodley, incidentally, who spoilt what I had long claimed to be a "world record" on my own part. He is the only person I have ever heard of who could claim, like myself, to have holed twice running with the same club without putting it back in the bag. The odds against this must be quite fantastic.

My own feat occurred at Letchworth. I sliced my brassie to the long 6th and holed from about 80 yards with a mashie, then repeated the process at the short 7th for a one. I well recall that, on taking the same club for my second at the next hole, I actually believed that I was more likely to hole out than not – such was the effect of the shock – while another part of my mind was saying "Later on you will be amazed that you could have thought what you're thinking now." Doing five holes in 3, 3, 1, 4, 3, I was out in 30 and then became so frightened that I took 39 to come home. This did not stop us celebrating that night in five different towns.

### THE THRILL OF IT ALL
One morning at Huntercombe a member come into the bar and revealed that he had just done the 6th in one. This is a hole in a slight dip, so that you can see the flag but not the hole. I held forth about the whole thrill of doing a hole in one lying in being able to see the ball go in.

In the afternoon, playing with Lord Banbury (which is irrelevant but serves to show how well connected I am), I hit an obviously good tee shot at the same 6th hole. He too was clearly on the green but, when we came up, only one ball was visible. He walked forward and picked mine out of the

In this series a complete
miss is well portrayed
Notice the divot marks of
previous toozhar, - also the
correct position of the hands

In No 2 the right elbow is
well raised, the body sways
back, & a determined look is
imparted to the face, whilst
the head is pivoted in the
direction of the hole.

No 3. Note the meticulous
care expended in maintaining
the correct angle of the club
face, - also the right leg
raised in anticipation of a
forceful blow

In the commencement of
the downward swing observe
the poise of the body on
the left leg, & the knee
& elbows well tucked out

The club head is travelling
so fast in No 5 that the
surprising result is registered
in illustration  Notice the
correct position of the eyes.
one on the club head, & the other
on the hole to be achieved in or so

Here the whole weight of
the body has been transferred
to the right leg, whilst the
left leg is commencing its
follow through

In this picture portraying
contact the nose is kept
well down & the new
Charleston movement is
typically exemplified

The swing is now nearly
complete, & the player's neck
is well pressed down & out, whilst
it will be seen that the lobe of
the right ear is kept immediately
over the knuckle of the right thumb

It might be supposed from
No 9 that the style is too
correct for an absolute airshot,
but the fallacy of this is proved
by reference to the ball which
remains triumphantly in situ

(1927)

hole. I had not even reached the green, so all I could do was to turn to the right and proceed to the next tee. It seemed to prove my point, I could not raise any excitement over it at all.

The most extraordinary near-miss was perhaps Jock Hutchison's in the first round of the 1921 Open, the one which he won after a replay with Roger Wethered. He holed the 8th in one and was stone dead for a two on the 9th, a full shot down-wind with a driver. As the ball approached some idiot of a spectator rushed forward and pulled out the flag. The handbook records that "the ball jumped over the hole and many onlookers thought that, if the spectator had not interfered, Hutchison might have achieved the unique feat of two successive holes in one."

At Deal many years ago a photographer asked Lionel Munn for an action photo – I have a strong feeling that it was actually for *Golf Illustrated* – whereupon he borrowed a club and ball and hit a shot from the 14th tee, and it went into the hole. The picture hangs in the clubhouse at Deal, and the action, caught at the moment of impact, is perfect. I often wonder whether it is the only photograph of a player actually doing a hole in one. (Editor's Note: No, not the only one. We published such a photograph in *Golf Illustrated* not so many months ago.)

The flukiness of the whole business is, I think, emphasised by the extraordinary difference in the numbers of holes in one done by the world's acknowledged masters, who spend their entire lives peppering short holes with iron shots. Sandy Herd, for instance, did 19 and for years the story went the rounds that an American was to present him with a gold putter when he did his 21st. He told me there was, alas, no truth in it and it all arose from a facetious remark at some dinner at Peoria, Illinois.

James Braid did 18 holes in one and J.H. Taylor ten, but the man who ought to have done the most was surely Harry Vardon. Yet he did only one. So, believe it or not, did Walter Hagen.

The handbook quotes many hole-in-one stories, of which I like particularly the one of Mr R. Slater, who drove from the 1st at Blackpool, hit the club flagstaff, and holed out at the 18th. Mr E.D. Stevenson in the Army Championship at Prestwick started with a ten and finished with a one, and Miss Gertrude Lawrence, the distinguished actress, it is declared, though I take it with a pinch of salt, "when playing golf for the first time, holed in one with her first tee shot".

All in all, the distinction of being the most fortunate holer-in one must surely go to my colleague, Leonard Crawley. A year or two ago he insured against a hole in one at Lloyds for £200; the premium was, I believe, £2 and it had to be done in a competition. Within a matter of months he had collected the money, free of tax, by holing in one in the German Open. (1961)

## Long Shots

When long shots are mentioned most golfers instinctively think of long tee shots, and it will not be disputed that the majority of the longest shots are struck from the tee.

Apart from the fact that more force is probably applied in hitting a teed ball than in the case of one resting on the ground, more full drive strokes are hit, even in these days of long courses, from the tee than from any other place, and it is therefore natural that more long shots are struck from the tee than "through the green".

The variations in the nature and state of the ground, and still more the force and direction of the wind at the place and time of the performances, render all statistics in this matter of but little service in comparing individual records, and probably for these reasons any statistics at all are difficult to come by. It may safely be said, however, that even with a following wind, a golf ball has rarely been driven much over 200 yards, all carry, or much over 300 yards carry and run combined, with wind and ground both favourable.

Long driving competitions are usually held under very favourable conditions, and it is the rarest exception for 200 yards to be exceeded by the winner, even with carry and run both counted.

While it is true that the longest drives of which there is any authentic records have been made from the tee, it by no means follows that it is not possible to drive equally long shots from a level lie on the fair green, and as a matter of fact, never having witnessed any of the record drives, we can affirm that some of the longest shots we have seen played have been struck from grassed lies.

### BIG BRASSIE SHOTS

A case in point happened in one of the rounds of the Open Championship at Hoylake in 1897. At the third hole, the length of which is 480 yards, Mr F.G. Tait's tee stroke finished up in the bunker which runs across the course

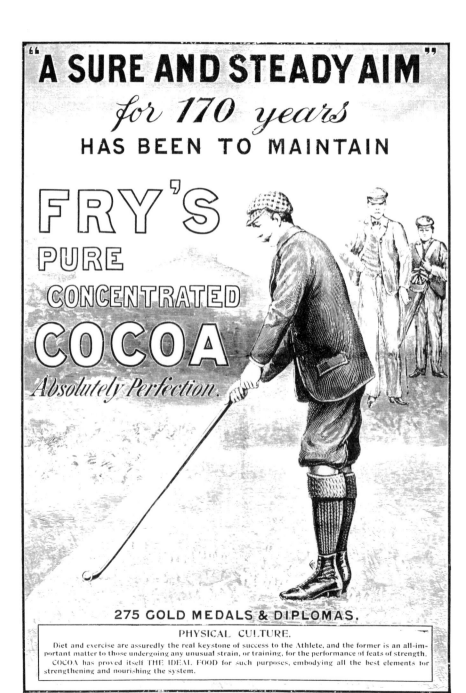

(1899)

about 200 yards from the tee. Mr Tait played forward with his niblick and only just got out, his ball resting about two yards in front of the bunker. He took his brassie and played a magnificent stroke, which carried about twenty yards over the bunker that guards the green, straight on the pin, and ran within six yards of the hole. His putt hit the back of the hole for four, but this brassie stroke must have carried at least 200 yards, for it was a high stroke and the ball had little run on it.

A very similar brassie stroke was played, curiously enough, also at Hoylake by Mr John Ball, jun., in the final of the Amateur Championship of 1894. The shot was played at what was then the 17th hole (now the 16th) from the corner of the field, and Mr Ball carried over the bunker and overran the hole. The distance was probably less than Mr Tait's stroke, but there was a slight wind against the player.

As everybody knows, Mr Tait is the hero of the longest tee shot of which there is any satisfactory record. He drove a ball from the Heather Hole at St Andrews to the Hole o'Cross, going homewards, a distance of 341 yards. The weather was calm but the ground was frozen. The carry alone is estimated to have been close to 250 yards.

Curiously enough the Hole o'Cross was the scene of another famous drive. Mr Samuel Messieux, who flourished at St Andrews about 1830, is reported to have driven a ball 380 yards from the Hole o'Cross into "Hell" bunker, but this feat is hardly sufficiently authenticated.

Some years ago Mr J.C. Baldwin, a well-known Edinburgh golfer and a long driver, informed the writer that on a frosty day he struck a ball from the third tee at Musselburgh, which was placed near the road which runs parallel with the course, all the way to "Mrs. Forman's". The ball struck the road and was found on it at a spot not far from the hole, a distance of about 400 yards.

## Harbouring the Finest Swing in Portugal

*David Davies*

Portimao, on the Portuguese Algarve, is a working harbour. It hosts dozens of beautifully coloured fishing boats, manned by swarthy and taciturn men who daily bring in the tons of sardines needed to fuel a fish-hungry populace, and business is brisk.

The sardines are stored in open compartments at the front of the 60 foot boats, swilling around with sea-water, and as the dockside is often six foot or more above the level of the deck the problem, in this labour-intensive land, arises of how to get them from the boat to the crushed ice boxes on the harbour.

The solution is a simple one. Four men form a human conveyor belt, one of whom clearly does not realise the potential that lies within him. He could be the new Doug Sanders, if, instead of slinging sardines, he turned his talents to golf.

Let me describe the unloading process. The men use small wicker baskets, with two small handles and the first of them scoops the fish out of the tank and hands it to the second man brimming with sardines and salt water. His problem then is to get the basket, with fish but without water, to the man on the harbour wall who is packaging them in ice.

He is six feet above him and 15 feet away and to take the three steps necessary and then hoist the basket upwards would obviously take so long that the sardines would be rotten by the time he had finished. So what does he do? He throws the basket, with incredible accuracy, straight into the hands of the man above him. To unload the boat completely may take two hours and in the course of that time our man will have thrown his basket of, say, 300 sardines, perhaps 1,000 times.

At the end of that time only a dozen or so sardines will have fallen on to the dockside, such has been his proficiency.

## DELICATE TOUCH OF THE BASKET MAN

The technique involved in this operation is both difficult and fascinating. It demands judgement of an extremely high order, it demands a delicacy of touch, it demands, above all, the ability to produce a repeating swing – and there, in that sentence you have the ingredients for a great golfer.

Let me attempt to describe a man who possesses, as near as dammit, the perfect swing and who has probably never heard of golf, let alone played it. The one I saw looked a little like Doug Ford, had the shoulders and wasp waist of Arnold Palmer and the Popeye forearms of Tom Watson.

He takes the streaming basket by both its handles and, using both hands and keeping it dead level, swings it smoothly back to just above waist height. The basket is taken back on the inside plane and is then swung forwards quite gently, allowing the weight of the sardines to generate enough speed to carry it through.

It is released at a point just after a golfer would have made contact with the ball and it then arches upwards in such a way that the two handles remain level with each other, the slippery sardines stay within the basket and the man on the dockside is presented with an easy catch. In order to achieve that flight the thrower not only has to pivot, he has to get through the ball, or basket, with his right hand, arm and shoulder in a way that would have the top class professionals drooling.

In 1970 I saw Sanders all but win an Open Championship with a swing that was not only shorter but was a good deal less smooth and, ultimately, less repetitive.

The boat does not stay in the harbour long and some of the shifted sardines travel 40 yards or so to Casa Bica, a dockside café, where the fish is grilled over charcoal burners in the open. The locals eat them whole, on a chunk of bread; the visitors are generally a bit more picky.

Some of them are refugees from the practice ground at the luxurious Penina Hotel, three or four kilometres up the road and have spent a frustrating morning belting ball after ball in search of the secret.

I have been one: I have done it, and I have never, in all the years, acquired even a semblance of the rhythm, the timing, the elementary grace of the unknown fisherman in Portimao who slings sardines for a pittance with a swing I would sell my soul for.

(1985)

The spiral shot.

(1892)

## Out on a Limb

*Chris Plumridge*

It has always struck me that God is probably not a golfer but, if He is up there knocking a ball around the Elysian Fields, then He doesn't think about the game too much.

The basis for this possibly controversial statement is founded on pure human observation. If God, as we are led to believe, made us in His image then He failed to realise that one day we might choose to pick up a stick and take a swipe at a pebble. This lack of foresight led Him to equip us with legs and arms of equal proportions, a pair of centralised eyes, a torso with an equal number of ribs and a number of joints and muscles which allow us to bend, twist and turn in all manner of directions.

While this combination makes for symmetry and allows us to perform ordinary tasks such as climbing Mount Everest, jumping a five-bar gate or simply unscrewing the cap of the gin bottle, when it comes to the business of hitting the pebble with the stick, it's utterly useless.

Doubtless the first man or woman to hit a pebble with a stick did so without thinking how it was done, but after a while, he or she would begin to wonder why the pebble couldn't be hit straighter and further. Other

" HOLD THE FLAG UP, CHARLIE "

pebble-hitters would gather round and exchange views and, in between inventing the wheel and discovering fire, would draw various conclusions as to what movements would make for straight and powerful hitting of the pebble. It would be at this juncture that the pebble-hitters would get the first inkling that their physiology was ill-designed for their requirements.

Today's golfer, the modern equivalent of those ancient pebble-hitters, faces much the same problem. God has persisted with His design and we find ourselves embarking on the job of hitting a golf ball still stuck with those symmetrical arms, legs, eyes, torso, muscles and joints. Thus equipped we find that in order to make an efficient pass at the ball we have to make one arm longer than the other, stiffen the joint in one arm, concave our chests and from the top of this contorted structure, peer at the ball through one eye like some half-witted Cyclops.

All of which brings me to Severiano Ballesteros. The current Open champion seems, on the face of it, a perfectly structured human being with an ability to overcome the sundry contortions golfers have to make and hit the ball with a freedom which leaves the watcher open-mouthed in wonderment. But now I can reveal to you the secret of Ballesteros' amazing success.

## WHY SEVE IS DIFFERENT

While dining with him recently the talk inevitably came round to the theories surrounding hitting a golf ball. 'How,' I asked, 'do you manage to hit the ball so far?' That question may seem trite since Ballesteros is built like a Pamplona bull but many bigger men still trail the young Spaniard, in length from the tee. Ballesteros said nothing in reply but simply stood up and asked me to study the length of his arms. Suddenly as he stood there, all was revealed. **With his shoulders perfectly level, Ballesteros' right arm was almost two inches longer than his left**.

The discovery of this physical phenomenon allowed everything to fall into place. While you or I, when addressing the golf ball, have to drop our right shoulder in order to place the right hand in the correct position on the grip and also check that, in doing so, we haven't pointed our shoulders left of the target, Ballesteros can get into the correct address position by virtue of a natural defect.

Come to think of it, just a hint of natural deformity may be the difference between being a good golfer and a champion. History can provide us with some excellent examples, not least of them being Ben Hogan. Hogan was,

~~~~~~~~~~~~~~~~~~~~~~~~~~~~~~~~~~~~~~~~~~~~~~~~~~~~~~~~

# THE
# OPEN GOLF CHAMPIONSHIP,
### *Open to all Golfers,*
## Will be played at PRESTWICK, on
# Wednesday & Thursday, 10th & 11th June next.

Names and Entrance Fee (£1 Amateur, 10s. Professional) must be received by the undersigned not later than Saturday, 6th June.

**MAJOR A. L. GALLIE,**

**Prestwick,**

Secretary, Prestwick G.C.

20th May, 1903.

(1903)

in his prime, regarded as the nearest thing to perfection in the art of striking a golf ball as is humanly possible or put another way, in the words of Gene Sarazen "Nobody covered a flag like Hogan." What may have given Hogan the edge over his contemporaries is the fact that he is naturally left-handed but chose to play golf right-handed. Johnny Miller is another who plays right-handed while being naturally left-handed and although his star has long since descended from the heights it scaled in the years 1973 to 1976, during that period he produced a brand of golf that bordered on the fantastic.

Could it also not be that Ed Furgol won the 1954 United States Open because of his withered left arm rather than in spite of it. Furgol's handicap was not a natural defect but the result of a childhood accident after which the arm was badly set and impaired. Although his left arm was too short and the muscles atrophied, it was permanently locked, thereby automatically allowing him to overcome a fault which plagues thousands of golfers.

Consider too the case of Vicente Fernandez, the 1979 PGA champion. He won that title at St Andrews playing through some of the vilest weather imaginable. But Vicente had one priceless advantage over his rivals – he was playing every stroke from a slight uphill lie simply because he was born with his right leg shorter than his left. Most golfers when playing from a slight uphill lie find themselves hitting a better shot than normal. Indeed

Douglas Bader who lost both legs in a pre-War flying accident, discovered the same. He was able to ensure himself a permanent uphill stance for every shot by simply sawing an inch or two from his right leg.

The real clincher to my theory, however, is none other than Jack Nicklaus. His edge over his rivals is not provided by any apparent physical oddities but via a more subtle route. Nicklaus is colour-blind. This may strike one as being a disadvantage until one considers that at most tournaments nowadays, the leader-boards show a player's figures in relation to under par scores in red. To Nicklaus, these figures appear black thereby providing him with the mental confirmation that he is far ahead of any other player in the field.

If God wants to produce the ideal golfer then He should create a being with a set of unequal arms and, likewise, legs, an elbow-free left arm, knees which hinge sideways, a ribless torso from which emerges, at an angle of 45 degrees, a stretched neck fitted with one colour-blind eye stuck firmly on the left side. And please God, let him be British.

(1985)

## HIAWATHA'S BRASSIE

Full of zeal, brave Hiawatha
Bought a brassie and a mashie,
Bought a bulger and a niblick,
Rolled his sleeves up and his trousers,
Paid a quarter to a caddie,
Winked at smiling Minnehaha,
Winked, and murmured, "Minnie, watch me!
Watch me when I wield my brassie,
Watch me beat this Auchterlonie
And these various famous Willies!
When I hit the ball I'll bust it,
Knock it into forty fragments,
Knock the pieces through the bunkers!
Stand aside, and let me waggle!"
In the sequel the "brave Hiawatha" foozled
his shot badly, as was to be expected.

[1905]

## A Talk With My Swing

*Eric Walmsley*

"Look, this game's important to me today. I want to win it badly. It all depends on you."

"*Does it really?*"

"Yes, it jolly well does. Now, no nonsense, mind. Slow back, no jerk, no sway, pivot, accelerate a bit and·then slam. Use the hands. Transfer the weight at the start of the down-swing. Don't fall over on the follow-through or use the club to prop me up or . . ."

"*I know how to suck eggs, thank you.*"

"I doubt it."

"*I beg your pardon?*"

"I said, 'I doubt it.' You know perfectly well what you've been doing lately. A prodigious great loop, a flopping of the wrists, a terrifying rigidity under pressure and a heaving of the right shoulder when playing irons off the tee. You're an absolute disgrace."

"*I see. And whose fault is that, may I ask?*"

"Yours, of course. You don't put your mind into your work.

"*I see. So if something goes wrong today, I shall get the blame, I gather.*"

"You most certainly will. If you don't do your stuff, I'm sunk – and that's that."

"*I see.*"

"And for heaven's sake stop saying, 'I see.' You're not a provincial magistrate."

"*There's no need to get abusive. If you must take out an insurance policy, you might at least do it civilly. After all, I do hold a position of considerable importance in your game. You should treat me with a proper respect.*"

"I would if you deserved it. The trouble is, you don't."

"*You used to like me once.*"

"That was before I saw those photographs. I know better now."

"*My practice swings are tremendously impressive.*"

"It's different when the ball's there."

"*Mine's not an easy job, you know. You're a pretty difficult person to work for. You're such an odd shape, for one thing. You've no idea the amount of sheer concentration I have to put in to get the club round your stomach. And those arms . . ..*"

"What's wrong with my arms?"

"So horribly out of proportion. And your neck . . . Rigid. Immobile . . . Is it any wonder I sometimes forget to bring the club-face square to the ball? It's a miracle I get there at all."

"Would you like some light clubs, perhaps?"

"No, thank you. I'm quite happy with the present ones. A most happy team, you might say. United in suffering . . . I'm sure you'll understand."

"I'll try."

"In fact, it looks as if you and I are stuck with each other. So we must try and make the best of it, mustn't we?"

"I'm afraid so."

"Well, off to work then . . . Now, what was it you wanted me to do? Straight right arm, shoulders stiff, out to it, hips locked . . . I know I can remember if I really concentrate . . . I know I can . . .."

(1959)

# THE GENERAL RULES OF GOLF

*Chris Plumridge*

I expect you have been wondering about the Meaning of Life. You know the sort of thing – why are we here, where are we going and is it possible to hit a 1-iron from a cuppy lie through a left to right cross-wind? Burning questions as to whether there is life after the lateral hip shift need to be answered if we are to find Peace and Eternal Happiness.

As a disciple of the Temple of the Ever Hopeful, I have spent many contemplative hours fasting on the top of a mountain (actually, it was the pulpit tee of the short 7th hole at my club but that's because Wednesday's child has vertigo), and my musings revealed the following *General Rules of Golf*.

The first tee shot following a lesson travels 20 yards along the ground.

The shortest distance between the ball and the target is never a straight line.

Electric trolleys break down at the furthest point from the clubhouse.

The pencil needed to mark a card is always at the bottom of the bag.

And when it is found, it is broken.

Immediately waterproofs are donned it stops raining.

Waterproof trousers cannot be removed without falling over.

When there is one minute left to get to the first tee, a shoe-lace breaks.

The ball nestling in a footprint in a bunker is always yours.

The only available space in the club car-park is furthest from the locker-room.

Rare mid-week rounds of golf take place in the midst of a visiting society.

The newer the golf ball, the greater its propensity for disappearing.

If the club is burgled, your clubs are never stolen.

And if they are, you are under-insured.

The reserve golf glove kept for wet weather has shrunk.

The number of practice balls recovered is always fewer than the number hit.

If you find your ball in the woods, it is unplayable.

If a professional finds his ball in the woods, not only is it playable but he can hit it on to the green.

The one remaining set of new clubs in the professional's shop was made especially for you.

Greens are hollow-tined and dressed the day before a competition.

In a pro-am, you are the last to drive off after your professional and partners have all hit screamers.

When you drive your car to a pro-am, you are caught in an impenetrable traffic-jam.

The latest piece of written instruction never works on the course.

The "yips" is something which afflicts other people.

Until now.

The sand in the bunkers is never the right texture for your particular method.

Television commentators invariably tell you what you can already see.

Someone always says "One" when your ball falls off the tee-peg.

The same person always says "Never up, never in" when you leave a putt of three feet short.

The same person always says "Why didn't you do that the first time?" when you hit a rasping stroke with a provisional ball.

The same person has to be led away before you fell him with your sand-wedge.

There is no truth in the theory that if you know how to shank you will never do so.

Passing lorry-drivers always shout "Fore" at the top of your backswing.

The best drive of the day finishes in a divot mark.

Delicate chips over bunkers always catch the top of the bank and fall back.

Out-of-bounds fences are located a foot the wrong side of your ball.

A hole-in-one is achieved when playing alone.

Whenever you take your clubs on a golfing holiday, you leave your game behind.

During the first round with a brand new set of clubs, the ball has to be played from a road.

Golf balls that are supposed not to cut have never been "thinned" out of a bunker.

Shots that finish close to the pin are never as close when you get there.

It's always the next round that will find you playing your normal game.

The General Rules of Golf affect only you.

(1985)

# CADDIE SCHOOL

## The Disappearing Caddie

*Henry Longhurst*

The gradual disappearance of the caddie from the golfing scene is to me a tragedy. I have enjoyed the company of caddies of all sorts and ages in roughly 26 countries and have always looked upon the relationship between the golfer and his caddie as one of the most rewarding things in the game – or so it has been, at least, to me.

I have always felt that it would be a fine thing for boys of all social grades to work their way up as caddies, as they do in the States. I can think of no better introduction to golf, quite apart from the benefit they would get from being in grown-up company in the sort of way that would not otherwise come their way. I know that in some clubs experiments have been tried in this direction, but they are rare exceptions.

Few golfers can afford to pay a pound per day for a caddie, though there must be hundreds who would willingly pay a boy ten bob – but boys don't seem to want ten bob these days, or girls either for that matter. I thought it was great fun during the French Open to see a mixture of grandmothers, grandfathers and teenagers of both sexes carrying the competitors' clubs and I should like to see it over here.

I was delighted to find during the Bowmaker Tournament at the Berkshire that I had been allotted the only female caddie. She was a young married woman and her name was Edith. The only fly in this particular ointment was that someone took her for my daughter! Edith told me that she often goes up to the Berkshire, travelling over by bus from her home at Bracknell, and that she found it all most interesting. Like a good caddie she took great pride in the fact that the last man she had carried for had won a competition.

### THE PUNGENT MRS STREAK

When I shared a cottage for some years after the war near Huntercombe, Mrs Streak, the greenkeeper's wife, often used to carry my clubs and I like to think we made a happy combination. Her pungent comments on the morals and eccentricities of some of the members would have shaken them if they could have heard!

Perhaps because I only carry a light bag I have had caddies of extreme ages, who could not have managed one of these modern cabin-trunk bags that so many people here, and all in America, seem to find necessary. The oldest was undoubtedly Mr Corstorphine, a valiant rubicund little figure who when he last carried my clubs in the Medal at St Andrews was well over 80. He had been in the Navy in the first war and had been discharged from the coastguards at the age of 72 in the second!

At the other end of the scale have been some of the nippers who have carried for me in the Halford Hewitt at Deal, including the one who got a whole story to himself in the _Daily Express_ by producing for me from the blouse of his miniature battle dress, when our fortunes were low, a huge slab of cake with pink icing. He had saved it up from the birthday party the night before, he said, when he had not gone to bed till ten. "Tst! Tst!" I said. I did not reveal to him when the last Old Carthusian had turned in.

(1957)

Golfing Dentist (absent-mindedly): " Quick, boy ! Give me the forceps ! We'll have this out
in half a jiffy ! "

(1912)

## YE CADDIE!

Who, at the golfer's soft behest,
Comes running with a short-lived zest!
Ye caddie!
Who starteth out with good intents
and seizeth bag and implements
Because he scenteth fifteen cents?
Ye caddie.

Who, at the start, keeps watchful eye,
And knoweth where the ball doth lie?
Ye caddie!
Who goeth soon into a trance,
Nor at the flying sphere doth glance,
But with our putter slayeth ants?
Ye caddie!

Who, not content with being blind,
Drags leisurely along behind!
Ye caddie!
And while the golfer at the tee
Waits for his driver angrily,
Who sleepeth on yon hill, care-free?
Ye caddie!

(1900)

Who ne'er with flag in hand is seen
Till all are waiting on the green?
Ye caddie!
Who telleth us the mode of play,
And grinneth if we go astray,
Until we long his hide to flay?
Ye caddie!

Who, when we wildly, vainly try
To leave a bunker's sand, doth guy?
Ye caddie!
Who doth our rival balls confuse,
And with our clubs himself amuse,
And our new balls for marbles use?
Ye caddie!

Who with suggestions bold doth teem
And maketh life a hideous dream?
Ye caddie!
Who loses three balls every day,
Yet waits, persistent, for his pay?
Whom do we often long to slay?
Ye caddie!

" Slower nor a flippin' Test Match !   Out in 53, 'e was—now 'e's battin' to save the follow-on ! "

# A Conversation Piece

*E.M. Prain*

It happened quite by accident. I entered the "Dog and Gun", ordered a pint, and sat down at a table near the bar counter. The only other occupant raised his eyes from his tankard, surveyed me with mild amusement as I took the first rapturous gulp. He was a somewhat unkempt man, and very bronzed. A soiled red handkerchief filled the hiatus caused by an open shirt, and the jaunty angle of his cap betokened self-respect and an optimistic outlook. With all the sedentary man's longing and envy I gazed at his sun-tanned skin, and instantly liked the open face which it adorned, and the bright twinkling eyes steadily appraising me. He must have read my thoughts.

"Thirsty weather, Guv'nor," he remarked cheerily. "And a bit of my sunburn won't do you no harm."

Agreeing readily on both counts, I explained that, chained as I was to the office stool, opportunity for enjoying the treats of Nature were limited.

"The open air for me, Guv'nor," he continued. "Oi couldn't stick no office stool."

"And what do you do for a living?" I inquired with interest.

"Well, Sir, Oi used to be an oitinerant caddie. But now, Oi reckons Oi'm a wanderin' weight-lifter."

Having heard of weight-lifters, but not wandering ones, I was curious.

"When did you change over?" I asked.

"Change over, Guv'nor? There weren't no change-over. It's all in the job now."

## A KICK IN THE PANTS, VERBAL LIKE

"You see," he continued, "when Oi'm workin', Oi carried 'atween 40 and 50 pounds for two and a 'arf-hours and Oi walks five miles in doin' it. At the finish, Oi gets two and a tanner, no applause and often a kick in the pants, verbal like. Blimey, Guv'nor, Oi've seen men at the 'Olborn Empire, what only raises the same for as long as it takes to down an 'arf pint in 'ot weather. All the customers gives them thunderin' applause, the Manager 'ands 'em twenty-five smackers an evenin', and there ain't a dame in the 'ouse what don't wish 'er 'usband or 'er sweet'art 'ad as much 'air on 'is chest. Oi'm askin' you, Sir; if them's 'E-men, what's the like of me?"

Cautiously avoiding the issue, I inquired how long my new friend had been a caddie.

"Thirty years," he answered proudly. "And Oi don't regret a day." Being an ignorant, though zealous golfer, I thought it might be interesting to have his views on the advance of golf.

"Well, what do you think of the game now?" I asked blandly.

At this, his face underwent a change. He leaned across the table and said fiercely:

"The game, Guv'nor, the game? That's the trouble – there ain't no game. It's a bloomin' business."

"But what do you mean by that?" I said, seeing more than a glimmering of the truth.

" **November days are dark and drear.** "

"You used to be able to tell a golfer by his clubs, Sir. If 'e 'ad seven or eight clubs in 'is bag, it were a blind certainty 'e could play. They was beautifully made, too. Each one a gem and indervidual like. Nowadays, what yer find? Norvices even, with a bag as big as yer cabin trunk and fourteen clubs beside. Four woods, Sir, and the rest is irons and putters, not to mention the Sandiron, and all graded as you might say. 'Caddie,' they says to me, 'These clubs 'as improved me game strokes. There's a club for each shot, and all you 'as to do is to swing in the groove like, and the bloomin' club will do the rest.'

"Now, Sir, what's the use o' fourteen clubs when you 'as fourteen grooves, and Oi'm not breathin' about the loops, kinks and sways. They're kiddin' 'im, Guv'nor, the blokes what manerfacters the clubs. They draws pretty designs on their faces – blue spots, red spots and all. Like the women these days; they daren't show their faces till they've 'ad a go with the paint. No, Sir, mass-perdition is the death of the game, and of the 'ole world by the looks of things."

"You sound very gloomy," I said, not entirely convinced. "What about the good golfer these days?"

## HIGH VELOCITY PELLETS

My companion paused. He took off his cap and replaced it at the same acute angle, lowered the contents of his tankard with a deep swallow and generally seemed to be playing for time. Then he began again.

"Oi'm not sayin' but what they're not good, Guv'nor. But Oi 'ate mechanical devices; and that's what they seems to me. No artistry, Sir, no 'arf shots, low 'ooks and 'oigh sloices, like what Taylor, Vardon, Braid, Ball and them done any day of the week. Oi carries twenty-odd clubs for 'em, and fifteen draws the bloomin' dole. Just a swipe and a No. 6, and they're on the green four 'undred an' fifty yards away as sure as Bob's yer uncle."

"They must be very long hitters," I ventured, with a hint of admiration. "The Old Timers couldn't do that, anyway."

For this remark I received the condescending look which the sophisticated sometimes bestow on the adolescent.

"No more they could even a few years back, Guv'nor," he continued. "We 'ad no high velocity pellets even that recent. Just a plain rubber core, what took an honest clout without flyin' away a bloomin' day's march out of sheer funk. Nowadays, there's them things as 'as needles an' 'oiperdermic

## "I'VE LEARNED THIS LESSON ABOUT GOLF

*Yes!*
*Steel*
*is*
*best*
*for*
*irons* "

"Yes, steel is best for irons. The new Master shaft has converted me, and I haven't recovered from my amazement yet at the wonderful improvement in my game. The ball leaves the club-head so sweetly too . . . goes off like a bullet. I'm playing far more seconds with irons now instead of wood. Much easier to do a lower score that way. I *feel* I'm going to make a good shot before I begin, instead of wondering where the ball was going, and hoping for the best . . . seem to have far more confidence and much more control as well."

"Yes, I'm finding that steel is best for irons, too. You know my handicap's just come down two strokes? Well, that's why!"

**TRUE TEMPER MASTER IRON SHAFTS** *for men in three grades of whip.*
**TRUE TEMPER IRONS** *specially designed for ladies.*

# TRUE TEMPER MASTER

### STEEL SHAFTS FOR IRON CLUBS

*True Temper Master Irons are made in a large variety of attractive finishes, Chromium, Black, light and dark grained enamel, light and dark sheath. Your pro. will gladly let you try them.*

*Players who prefer the* **TWIN TAPER** *type of shaft can now obtain* **TRUE TEMPER** *Woods and* **TRUE TEMPER** *Master Irons in this form.*

Made for BRITISH STEEL GOLF SHAFTS LTD., of 26, EXCHANGE STREET, EAST, LIVERPOOL, by ACCLES & POLLOCK LTD., of OLDBURY, BIRMINGHAM

(1933)

syringes. They're shoutin' for a larger ball, Sir. Blimey, it'll be 'ere any time; they must 'ave room to pack the dynermite."

"The more the better," I rejoined with feeling. "Soon I'll be driving our long three-shotter." Even the thought was enough to produce a pleasant sensation down the spine.

"It's 'oigh time the Minister of Agriculture done somethin'," added my friend, completely ignoring my sally.

I was mystified, and said so.

"The golf courses is takin' up all the arable land, Govnor," he explained. "You take a piece of elarstic and stretch it with both 'ands. Then you 'as what's going on in Golf to-day. Yer left 'and is the bloomin' ball and yer right the tee-in' grounds. Every year yer ball flies further, and what 'appens? The Club Committees 'ires an architec', what goes prospectin' in the Bush. If 'e don't lose 'isself, back 'e comes, proud as Punch, to tell us we tees up somewhere in no man's land. Yer'll soon 'ave to 'ave yer passport visa'd if you wants to play at all."

"What'll be the end of it all?" I asked, impressed by the gravity of the situation.

"'Strewth, Sir, Elijah would be 'ard pressed to say. But Oi reckons the time ain't far away when Yorkshire won't be no county, only the first nine 'oles of the Championship course!"

At this, I think I must have blenched; for, in the same breath, the prophet added:

"Now 'ave one with me, Guv'nor?"

I did. It was a whole pint, and I needed it.

(1938)

## Dog Caddies

_John Milne_

The rule excluding dogs from golf links is probably one universally adopted by golf clubs, and yet perhaps the following notes of a dog caddie may suggest, for certain links at least, the expediency of more elasticity being imported into the rule, or, at least, some modification of its stringency.

"Billie", the subject of this little sketch, is regarded as an honorary member of the club to which I belong, as a teacher of morality to human caddies, and as a successful finder of golf balls, so that whenever I go golfing, whether I have a caddie or whether I am unfortunate to be without one, dog Billie goes also. Of course, there is the rule, blindly copied from the rules of other clubs, that such a procedure entails a fine, but as Billie has proved himself to be so useful to both players and caddies, and at the same time added new interests to the sport, up to date the penalty has never been enforced.

Billie – and no doubt other dogs have done the same – learned all that a dog wants to know about golf in five minutes. He finds balls, retrieves balls, keeps to heel, and doesn't touch a ball in play. Should a ball go over a fence which is high and thick, or on which there is a notice-board that trespassers will be prosecuted, a very small hole suffices for Billie, and the ball comes back. You haven't had your face scratched in a thorn fend, you have had the pleasure of seeing Billie hunt, saved a possible summons, saved time, saved a bob, and saved a temper, and having saved the last you have possibly saved a game.

Frequently both players and caddies are astonished by a ball being found twenty or thirty yards away from the place it was supposed to be, and it is a very rare occurrence for a ball to be lost. On the contrary, you may return with more balls than you started with; and a box of balls that never empties is as comforting as the widow's cruse.

## BILLIE'S IDEAL COURSE

When Billie sees a good drive he gives a grunt and distinctly smiles, but he doesn't care for good play. What he likes best is to go with a couple of bad players over a sporting course. Let there be nothing but blind drives, a few pits and quarries, lots of fences, ditches, gorse patches, ponds and brooks, and Billie will golf all day. Then there is something for a dog to do, and the players may come home with a bigger collection of balls than they possessed at starting, and instead of being depressed and saying that they will give up the game – a course which has been followed by many an embryonic player – will go at it again next day.

When Billie's services are regarded in this light, he and his kind – and no doubt there are many other dog caddies in the world – have done more than a little to encourage a healthy sport and trades connected with same. A healthy body means a healthy mind, and for success in this world an equipment of common sense and good manners, which are largely derived from intercourse in sport, are worth all the lore of universities and schools.

Whenever I stand in a biting wind blocking the way for those behind whilst a "foozler" in front is poking about for a lost ball I feel that if there should be a fine about dogs it should be imposed on those who failed to bring one. When Billie goes out I never keep them behind anathematising, or expect to hear an opponent cheerfully reminding me that lost ball means lost hole.

Lastly, there is the moral influence that Billie exercises. When a caddie sees a clean new ball tucked away in a tussock of grass, the temptation not to discover it until a later period has frequently been irresistible. Another, but less rare, temptation to a caddie is to walk behind a player with a hole in his pocket. When a ball drops out, he picks it up and sells it to its owner. Billie evidently does not sympathise with these bad habits, so pounces on the ball himself.

(1979)

"**Roars of approval, sounds ominous. You're probably bunkered.**"

## SCOURGE OF BALL-SNEAKERS

These, however, do not exhaust the whole of Billie's virtues. On more than one occasion I have come up to a little gathering of ragamuffins loitering about bushes and ditches near the place where a ball must have pitched. Of course, they say they never saw it, or possibly that they heard it drop in a bank which they kindly indicate. Experience has taught me and others that the ball will next be played with by some stranger who has purchased it for two-pence. Billie declines to hunt in the bank, but instead looks inquiringly at the innocent faces of what we now know to be juvenile ball-sneakers; and as it is known that he can now pick out the youth that has the ball in his pocket, ball-sneaking is on the wane.

Once I heard about Billie's vices. An opponent declared that he went ahead and teed up his owner's ball – a charge utterly groundless, as shown by his owner's scores.

It must not be imagined that Billie is taking the bread out of a poor caddie's mouth. Whenever a caddie can be found he is engaged, and as he receives in addition to the usual pittance balls which Billie may have come across lost by previous players, Billie and caddie are particularly chummy. As he helps your partner and anxious searchers you may pass, he is also welcomed by every member in the club. Since January 1st his record day was twelve balls – which means that in a very few hours he paid his tax and had something to his credit.

Now, all that I have here said is not that Billies are required on every course, for there are courses where you could not lose a ball even if you tried; but that on many courses where caddies are scarce and difficulties are

**NEVER SAY DIE.**
GOLFER (*who is four down and five to play, to Caddie*).—" Here, take my club ; I'll give up the match ! "
CADDIE.—" Ah ! dinna gie it up ; the ither man micht dee ! "

numerous, the value of a good ball-finder is distinctly great. In the rules for such links references to fines for dogs should only apply to untrained beasts.

Trained dogs might easily become a source of revenue.

Of course, many may say that a trained dog is expensive and that a sporting dog with a good nose is required – statements far from being true.

As raw material, almost any sort of dog will do – a half-crown dog or the first coyote you meet in the street. First train him to come to heel. To do this you don't pound the dog with a niblick, or he may become links-shy. Talk to the beast gently, and when he is at heel give him a bit of biscuit.

Secondly, teach him the bread-and-butter trust trick, until he will even drop a piece of biscuit.

After this, let him run after a golf ball, which he must drop on hearing the word "trust," or its equivalent.

Lastly, and this is the most important, give the dog something to smell: before you tee your ball _wipe it on a cleaner on which you have placed a few drops of oil of aniseed._

Do this, and you will save money, save time, save your temper, save invectives, play more golf, get better health, improve the morality of caddies, and destroy incentives to trifle with the eighth commandment.

(1903)

## What is a Caddie!

To the Editor of _Golf Illustrated_

Sir, What is a caddie?

The ordinary golfer will probably reply that he is a person who carries his clubs and tenders him advice about the game, often superfluous, and owing to his – the golfer's – own inherent incapacity, usually useless.

The Commissioners of St Andrews, however, have other views of the caddie's nature and attributes. They are reported to have defined him officially as "a person who is licensed, wears a badge, is decently clothed and strictly sober."

Somebody once defined a professional golfer as "a man who spits on his hands," and one is almost forced to the conclusion that this person must have been a St Andrews Commissioner in embryo. As a definition, except on the _lucus a non lucendo_ principle, the present example is ludicrous in the extreme.

Like the St Andrews definition of a stroke, the Commissioners' definition of a caddie is no definition at all. It merely mentions a few attributes, of chiefly negative import, of the thing defined, and contains no definite or complete information about it.

Let me examine for a moment the pronouncement, such as it is, of the St Andrews Commissioners. It is clear, in the first place, that no person is caddie unless he wears a badge or is licensed. Against this reduction of the free and independent caddie of the Royal and Ancient Game to the level of the street porter, or the ordinary cabman, I desire to protest.

Can any one imagine "Fiery", or "Big Crawford", *wearing a badge?* and would any St Andrews Commissioner dare to affirm at a *confrontation* with either of those gentlemen that he was not a caddie?

## DECENTLY CLOTHED AND STRICTLY SOBER

But let me proceed. A caddie is not a caddie, within the meaning of the Act framed by the St Andrews Commissioners, unless he be "decently clothed". It is not for a moment to be supposed that the St Andrews Commissioners mean to insinuate that the St Andrews caddies have been in the habit of offering their services to the golfers in any indecent attire; but the question is, what do the St Andrews Commissioners mean by decent clothing? Do they exclude bare feet and ankles, or even knees? Do they draw the line at rent or patched garments, or insufficient linen? In short, what *do* they mean?

If the St Andrews Commissioners use the word "decent" in its aesthetic sense of a perception of fitness and proportion, their legislation had more properly been directed against the golfer than his caddie. The latter, so far as I have observed, is at least always clothed according to his means and station.

But the crowning insult to the caddie is the last. A caddie is not a caddie unless he is "strictly sober". Again, it may be asked, what is "strictly sober"? I make bold to state that, on the green, I have seen more caddies "strictly sober", especially after lunch, than I have seen golfers. I say this in no sense of impugning the sobriety of golfers, who, indeed, are remarkable for the temperance which they exhibit in their pursuit of the most trying and thirst-producing of all sports. But I wish to protest against this additional insult to a deserving class of men, a class which, in this respect, compares more favourably with any other.

It is difficult to see why a golf caddie should be subjected to these indignities. He is amenable to the ordinary laws of the land. Unlike a pedlar, or a cabman, there is small danger in the event of transgression of his being able by sudden departure to evade punishment. Should he misbehave himself the matter is soon common knowledge on the links, and he suffers punishment in lack of custom. But the crowning condemnation of the modern system of official control is that it destroys almost entirely the independent spirit and the original character of the caddie, which, up till lately, have had free scope, and have formed not by any means an insignificant part of the charms of golf.

I am, Sir, etc.,
An Old Golfer

(1899)

**SANDY VARDON: "Ere, Miss, you watch me."**

# MY CADDIE

Who daily comes to meet my trap,
And – touching jerkily his cap –
Seizes umbrella, clubs, and wrap?
My Caddy.

Who makes a little sandy tee,
And, down upon his bended knee,
Adjusts the Golf-ball carefully?
My Caddy.

Who, if I make a decent hit,
Is sure to let me hear of it?
Who flatters me a little bit?
My Caddy.

Who, when the balls erratic fly,
Can always an excuse supply,
"The stance was bad," or else "the lie?"
My Caddy.

Who if to pieces I should fall
And top, and pull and slice the ball,
Knows better than to talk at all?
My Caddy.

Who, when from hazard blind and bad,
He telegraphs the signal glad –
"All clear", becomes "a clever lad"?
My Caddy.

But who, if it should come to pass
The ball is lost in whins or grass,
Too frequently becomes "an ass".
My Caddy.

Who, if I suffer from "a rub",
Or badly lie in sand or scrub,
Had *better* hand the proper club?
My Caddy.

Who, when I'm down a hole or two,
Has sometimes all that he can do
A weary task to worry through?
My Caddy.

Who, though I hurry through the green,
Should ever at my heels be seen,
Attentive, tireless, and keen?
My Caddy.

Who, when the foe walks proudly in,
Is heard to swear through thick and thin
That luck alone has let him win?
My Caddy.

Who, ever anxious to defend
My interests from end to end,
Ought to be treated as a friend?
My Caddy.

(1891)

*Maurice Noel*

# DOCTOR'S ORDERS

## A Pathology of Golf

*E.H. King*

In treating of the diseases of golf in a small compass it is necessary for the benefit of our readers that we should take only those cases which have hitherto received too little attention in the medical world. Naturally, we take first in order that particularly distressing complaint **(1) Joceo capitis**, or throwing up of the head. This disease, while common in most young players and liable to be contracted at any period of the game, is especially noticeable when addressing the ball on the tee. The first symptom is a convulsive movement of the hands and an uneasy shifting of the feet, which is often followed in the case of nervous patients by a reddening of the face and a desire to shun the public gaze. A cure can sometimes be effected by plenty of club swinging exercises or the wearing of a martingale, but the patient would be advised to put himself in the hands of a professional man.

It is often followed by a severe attack of **(2) Laceratio pillulis**, or topping of the ball. This disease is one of the most common known to medical science, and is attributable often to an excessive indulgence in alcohol, but more frequently to a desire to watch the flight of the ball. The best known remedy for this complaint, when not accompanied by **Jaceo capitis**, is to substitute luncheon with liqueurs by a high tea.

**(3) Blasphemitis**, or loosening of the tongue. This is a most painful malady, commonly supposed to result from a long sojourn in hot climates, though it is frequently known to follow after a bad stroke (*foozlum*). The symptoms manifest themselves in a sudden reddening of the cheeks and neck (**Blushio choleris**), and are always followed by a profuse suppuration of bleeding matter from the mouth. No cure of this disease is known to medical men, and it can be said to end only at death.

Akin to it, but not always accompanied by fatal results, is **(4) Caddidamitis** a milder form of **Blasphemitis**. This is a latent but not a troublesome affliction, unless aggravated by **Actio stupidionem**, a disease prevalent among caddies. Much can be done to alleviate the patient addicted to **Caddidamitis**, by surrounding him with refined female society. Above all, he should endeavour to avoid becoming overheated.

(1892)

(5) **Congestio linkorum,** or crowded course. This aggravating complaint is very common in summer and amounts almost to an epidemic. The patient complains first of a sense of fullness and oppression, then of an acute nausea of his surroundings, and perhaps a slight deafness. All may be well if his partner can distract his attention from himself. But not infrequently these symptoms, without any "fore"-warning, are followed by a severe pain in the back which causes convulsive movements of the arms. If these should bring on an attack of **Blasphemitis,** the patient often feels greatly relieved, and is sometimes able to continue his game undisturbed.

**(6) Submergio pillulis**, or rabbit scrape, is one of the few diseases of golf that require surgical treatment. It affects patients in different ways, but it is almost invariably accompanied by a violent irritability, restlessness, and a sense of loss. In troublesome cases the patient is seized with a sudden dejection, and wanders aimlessly about with his eye fixed on the ground in front of him. To effect a complete cure, after the seat of the trouble has been located, the affected part must be cut away with a niblick, but care should be taken to replace the surrounding tissues (_divotti_) to give the wound a chance to heel. The operation must be performed with the greatest skill and should not be attempted after mortification has set in, or **Laceratio pillulis** is likely to supervene. A partial cure can be effected by a "pick-me-up", but this treatment invariably results in another stroke (_penaltium_) and is not recommended.

(1912)

## When Golfers Should Know Better

### Henry Cotton

Is golf a dangerous game for the over forties? It is stated four men died on the links during one weekend none older than 56, and four more collapsed. This was the theme of an article I read recently and the writer went to the trouble to collect together all sorts of opinions. You do not hear of people dying playing tennis, the writer states. I think if people of the same physical condition and age as the average golfer played tennis they would die like flies.

I do not think many people really try seriously to take the maximum care of their most precious worldly possession – their health. They just live on without caring and indulging heavily under the "one only lives once" slogan. I should say that old golfers would consider that golf has added years to their lives. There are always a few who try to do too much anyway, even if it is gardening or painting the house, and to play golf perhaps pulling a trolley on an exhausting day on an exhausting course when already tired is not sensible even if one is 30 not 50!

One should know better. If I had listened to my wife I would not have played in the final two rounds of Muirfield this year. She kept saying she could see I was tired out. I did 77s and did not seem to be playing badly. I suppose it was just general fatigue.

(1959).

# The 'Great' British Breakfast

*Peter Dobereiner*

Why do British golfers not do better on the Continent? That seems to be the question of the hour. Leave aside for the moment the fact that British players have captured two out of the four European Championships played so far this season. The pundits are asking why we don't do better and when pundits ask it behoves us all to pay attention and come up with an answer.

The question itself is interesting, not so much because it is irrelevant, but because of its splendid imperial assumptions. The thinking behind the question clearly goes like this: British golfers who are – naturally – the best, play on the Continent against foreigners who, by definition, are inferior. How is it possible, then, for a foreigner ever to prevail in such a contest?

That type of arrogance was what made the British Empire great. Such thinking provided the civilising force which carried Anglo-Saxon culture around the globe. The minute anyone questioned this God-given superiority of the British then the entire Empire collapsed in ruins.

## BRITISH INFALLIBILITY

Just imagine what a shambles there would have been if the Duke of Wellington had ever wavered in his faith in the infallibility of the British. Today we would be calling our rubber boots "Napoleons", or "nappies", and Waterloo would be a station on the Paris Métro. Unthinkable. Thank goodness golf has not succumbed to the effete doctrine that all men are born equal. We can press on with the question why British golfers do not do better.

I have spent many years researching this problem and am now able to reveal my findings in a word. Breakfast. More properly, we should use several words, such as *café complet, piccola colazione or pequeño almoco*.

Your average British professional golfer is a creature of habit. He is accustomed to rise in the morning, go to the hotel dining room and immerse himself in the sports pages of one of the more lurid morning papers. When the waitress appears at his side with the customary enquiry "Whaterwant?' the golfer replies "Georgie".

For those who have not been employed as commercial travellers and are therefore not conversant with the argot of British hotels, I will explain the relevance of this exchange. "Watcherwant?" translates as: "Good morning,

The Open-air Smoker finds that Three Nuns meets all his requirements. It burns slowly and evenly, the ash does not blow in the strongest wind, each pipeful is cool and sweet to the bottom of the bowl. And the quality and fragrance never vary.

THREE NUNS TOBACCO

(1924)

Sir. I hope you slept well and are enjoying your visit. May I have the pleasure of taking your order for breakfast?"

"Georgie" is less obvious. It is a reference to George Best, whose last name in dining-room shorthand, BEST, stands for Bacon, Eggs, Sausages and Tomatoes.

## WAITRESS'S NIGHTMARE

Last season we had a variation in this ritual. I am not sure who started it, but several golfers used the ploy before the year was out. Having given his order the golfer set aside his newspaper and expanded on the theme: "I would like the sausage charred black on one side and red raw on the other. The egg should not only be fried to the consistency of an ice-hockey puck but should furthermore be vulcanised to the plate. The bacon should consist entirely of fat and be merely lightly warmed. Likewise the tomato should be both green and raw. And the plate must be swimming in grease."

Inevitably, the harassed waitress who has been scribbling in her pad

If you foozle with your cleek,

And your putts are—let's say— weak ;

If your drives, for all to see,

Do not always leave the tee,

And to slice them is a habit—

If, in short, you are a rabbit,

Do not put your clubs away—

Drink a Guinness every day.

(*Guinness is, we'd like to add,*

*Good for those who aren't so bad.*)

## A Guinness a day is good for you

replies along lines: "I'll see what I can do, sir. I am not sure if the chef can manage it exactly like that." "Nonsense," says the golfer. "Just tell him to do it like he did yesterday."

Perceptive readers will have tumbled to the conclusion which has taken me so long to distil from my researches. The British golfer likes to go to work in the traditional style of the condemned man, with a hearty meal under his belt. And routine, as we all know, is the key to golf.

But what happens when this golfer goes to the Continent? No Georgie Best. No chance. He cannot even get an early morning cup of tea in bed and for those of us whose waking moment is a matter of extreme delicacy, with life itself hanging by a thread, the absence of the restoring brew is extremely serious.

## STRAIGHT INTO ATTACK

At the French Open I decided to strike a blow for the British way of life and went straight into the attack. As I booked in at the modern, international hotel I announced firmly: "I like a cup of tea in my room in the morning. No croissant, vous comprenez, and none of those rolls which are so crisp they chip the enamel off your teeth. I do not require a sachet of apricot jam nor a refreshing glass of saccharine and citric acid. Just a plain, honest-to-goodness cup of tea. Belly varnish. Rosie Lee. Le thé anglais. Can you ride tandem?"

The girl looked at me as if addressing an idiot child and said in perfect English: "I quite understand. There is an order form in your room. If you can manage to fill it out correctly you will get your tea."

She was right about the order form. It took the form of a multiple choice examination paper. You had to tick the appropriate box from a selection of "Tea with Milk", "Coffee without milk", "Tea with rolls", "Coffee with lemon" and so on. I painstakingly completed the questionnaire and fell back exhausted onto the bed, failing to hang the document on the door-knob of my room. Thus the morning dawned, without tea, and it took me three goes to sort out which shoe went on my right foot.

The second evening I took the challenge seriously. I was abstemious with the after dinner brandy in order to keep my mind razor sharp for the late night ordeal with the exam paper. I filled it out meticulously, checked and rechecked my answers and hung the form on my door. Mortal man could do no more to ensure a prompt supply of the reviving Lapsang.

## VICTORY AT LAST

The girl entered bearing a tray with a huge selection of the baker's craft, jams and butter and a pot containing a tepid, purplish liquid which, with extreme charity, I took to be coffee. I registered a reproof at the reception desk. They loyally insisted that I must have made a mistake in my order. I stood my ground. They sent for the order form and duly acknowledged that the mistake was theirs. Consternation. Such a thing had never happened before. The culprit would be sought out and severely reprimanded. Tomorrow, I could rest assured, all would be well.

As indeed it was. The tray contained a cup, milk, sugar and a pot of tea. Nothing else. Formidable! It is odd how such a small success looms as a major triumph. With much the same excitement as Jason must have felt with he saw the golden fleece within his grasp I reached out a trembling hand – and knocked the tray onto the floor.

As for the breakfasts, well I believe that a few persistent souls did actually achieve a boiled egg which, for some reason, took forty minutes to prepare. Most of them had to play on coffee and rolls and most of them, as we know, did not win the championship. You find my diagnosis suspect? Well, just consider this fact. The winner was Peter Oosterhuis and he was guest for the week at the British Embassy, probably the one place in France where they know the meaning of a decent bacon and egg breakfast.

(1974)

EVERY GOLFER AND ATHLETE should take
# TEESHOT BITTERS.

which ensures good play.

Invaluable for good driving

Regd.
TRADE

Regd.
MARK.

An unfailing Invigorator,

and steady putting.

A FEW DROPS OF THE "TEESHOT" BITTERS.
In Water, Wine, or Spirits, taken before meals, will stimulate the appetite, clean the palate; and, without discolouring, impart an agreeable and pleasant flavour to any liquid
A teaspoonful in water keeps the mouth moist, obviating entirely that feeling of dryness in the throat so distressing to those engaged in violent athletic exercise.
*Wholesale Agents:* **BARCLAY & SONS, Farringdon Street, LONDON, E.C.**
*Bottle, post free,* **3s.**

(1891)

## Lacerated Fingers

To the Editor of *Golf Illustrated*

Sir, As a beginner at the game I am faced with a great discomfort. When playing, the tips of my fingers become lacerated, and by the time I have turned for home blood is dripping from them!

Could any reader tell me the cause of this? I have tried wearing gloves, but that, apparently, made matters worse.

I am, Sir, etc.,
Sufferer
(1903)

## Accidents at Golf

At this holiday season, when the links are crowded with players, golfers cannot be too careful lest they endanger the lives of others by undue keenness over their strokes or through impatience at delays.

We should not envy the feelings of any player who killed a fellow-creature, either by a reckless stroke, or, still worse, by a stroke played in a passion at some vexatious delay.

In America, hardly a week passes without three or four golfing accidents – of which a large proportion are fatal – being reported in the papers. In this country casualties on the links are comparatively rare; whether because we exercise greater care or are more fortunate, is perhaps open to question. It may at least be affirmed that there is a great deal of carelessness and thoughtlessness in this respect among golfers, for which, in my view of the serious risks involved, it is hard to find any excuse. But the recklessness and thoughtlessness are not confined to the players. The onlookers at a big match have a habit of crowding so closely on the players and on the line of play, that it is little short of miraculous and that serious accidents are not quite common.

The pace of a golf ball during the first hundred yards or so of its flight is so enormous that instant death would necessarily be the fate of anyone who received a blow on the head, and yet the players frequently strike their tee shots down a solid lane of human beings all craning their necks out as if for the special purpose of inviting the blow!

It is high time that some more stringent measures were adopted for regulating the movements of the huge crowds that now attend golf matches, no less in the interests of golf than of public safety. But probably until somebody gets killed the present exceedingly inadequate arrangements will continue.

(1899)

## Athletic Heart

The doctors are trying to frighten us again. Witness this:

"Ninety-six per cent of the young men today have cardiac hypertrophy, or the athletic heart", according to testimony given in the Supreme Court yesterday by Dr Edward E. Hicks.

Dr Hicks had been appointed to examine Bernard Nelson, who is suing the Union Railroad Company for $15,000, and who bared his chest on Monday afternoon and made his heart-throbs an exhibit in the case.

Dr Hicks examined Nelson in the court-room. He then went on the stand and testified that there was a rapid heart, but no heart murmur or regurgitation. He was asked if cardiac hypertrophy was a serious ailment, and he said:

"No, I should not say so. Ninety-six per cent of the young men of today have it. It is a thickening of the heart muscles, due to golf, baseball, and other athletic exercises."

(1903)

# NATURE TRAIL

## The Advantage of Rabbits

In the course of a very interesting article in the *The Field* in defence of the rabbit on the links the writer asks: "Is it really the case that the rabbit is the enemy of the golfer? He is legislated for in the code of rules applying to all seaside links, and in this respect he seems to claim perhaps a larger share of the attention of golfing legislators than the humble position he occupies in the scheme of nature would seem to warrant. The little mark on his paws, like the mark of Bill Smith on the marriage register before the days of the all-pervading school-boards and a system of free education, is to be found with irritating frequency on the majority of seaside putting greens; and those golfers who have found their ball lying in one of these scrapes, either on the course or on the putting green, are not likely to be induced to entertain a feeling of tenderness towards the presence of the rabbit on the links, especially when his little peccadilloes have contributed to the losing of an important match.

Yet there are aspects from the golfers' point of view which really seem to prove that, broadly considered, the rabbit on the links is more the friend than the enemy of the golfer. This contention does not mean that the presence of the rabbit on the links should be welcomed in hordes and devastating battalions. That condition of affairs undoubtedly means golfing anarchy.

But the rabbit, when viewed with a kindly eye, is really the golfer's best greenkeeper. The razor-like saws of his teeth crop the grass into a finer texture of light and closely-knit turf than any species of machine lawn mower which can be constructed by human ingenuity. Its operations as a turf mower, carried over a long period of time, and with a zeal and energy that know no abatement either in winter cold or summer heat, prepare a kind of turf for the golfer which no hand labour of the most skilful greenkeeper can possibly produce.

If proof of the rabbits' operations in this respect are needed, one has only to point to a few of the principal golf courses in the country in order to show that it would not be any paradoxical claim to make that those greens which

# A Plant Worth Looking After!

HAVE YOU GIVEN <u>YOUR</u> LITTLE BIT?

(1927 - On fund-raising to send the Ryder Cup team to America).

stand highest in the golfer's estimation to-day, mainly on account of the fine lies to be met with on their turf, are really due to the thorough grazing work of the rabbit. Centuries ago, when St Andrews and Montrose were played upon by the lairds and nobility of Scotland, when the great Montrose sought a relaxation from his wars and the tedium of his honeymoon in playing golf both at St Andrews and Montrose, the links in those days were really communal rabbit warrens. There are historical documents extant to prove that the St Andrews course, when it belonged to the ancient municipality, was a source of great profit to the town by being leased for rabbits; and the same remark holds good with regard to nearly every one of the principal seaside greens in Scotland whose history in ancient times was linked in a manner, however imperfect, with the local self-government of the neighbouring village community.

## CHEWED TO THE TEXTURE OF VELVET

The great charm, for example, of St Andrews to the visiting golfer, who has heard something of its ancient story in history, and of the unequalled character of its golf, has lain very largely in the exquisite quality of its turf. In days when everyone plays golf, sometimes with the rude and scarring iron only, the beautiful turf of St Andrews, North Berwick, Carnoustie, Montrose, Troon, and Prestwick is in danger of being destroyed beyond the powers of recuperative redemption, owing to the crowds that swarm over these links in the holiday seasons. But the origin of the fine quality of the turf that used to be found in these places for the recreative pastime of the golfer was produced neither by greenkeeper nor lawn mower, but by the many thousands of rabbits that applied their sharp, little teeth in cropping the turf into a fineness of texture almost corresponding to velvet. If, moreover, any golfer wishes to see the most perfect and natural turf produced solely by the agency of the rabbit, let him pay a visit to the private green of Archerfield, in East Lothian. The golf course attached to the mansion house is laid out upon a rabbit warren.

There must be hundreds of thousands of rabbits burrowing on the wide strip of land that stretches from the mansion of Archerfield to the rocky seashore opposite to the Island of Fidra. It is true that a sliced or pulled ball two out of three times finds its destination in a cluster of perplexing rabbit holes, and often a straight shot on the course itself leaves the ball lying in the deep sandy rut of a fresh rabbit scrape. Those are the exasperating or exhilarating incidents of the game when played over a territory wholly given up to rabbit colonisation, and where no set policy has been adopted to deal with the rabbit with the thoroughness which the majority of golfers advocate as the true policy to be adopted. That, however, is not the aspect of the problem which has to be considered. The fact remains beyond question that the turf as left by the rabbit is the very best that can be conceived for the purposes of golf. The grass is extremely fine and close, giving a perfect lie in the way of a teed ball for a wooden club in the second shot.

The putting greens seldom need the lawn mower, for the rabbits that come out in thousands in the gloaming nibble the grass laden with the fresh evening dew, and leave it almost as closely cropped as if it had been shaved with a razor."

(1906)

## A Coarse Guide To Golf's Horticultural Bent

*Chris Plumridge*

Golfers with a horticultural bent derive great pleasure from watching the US Masters on television. April always finds the famed Augusta course decked in its most flamboyant colours as azaleas, magnolias and other sundry trees and shrubs burst forth in early season splendour. However, nature's bounty is not merely confined to the rolling terrain of the Georgia course and the golf courses of the world are inhabited by many rare and exotic species which are worth closer examination.

This brief guide tells you what look for as well as providing information on pruning techniques, weed and pest control.

**Nicklaus Jackmanii** (Ursus D'Oro): Popularly known as the Ursus D'Oro, the Nicklaus Jackmanii has, for many years, been the dominant plant in the plot since it superseded the perennial favourite, **Latrobe Delight** (Palmeris Chargum). Other plants, such as **Miller's Flash** (Mormonia) and **Kansas Star** (Watsonia), have tried to outgrow the Ursus D'Oro and have enjoyed brief spells of popularity but the influence of this plant and the spread of its branches has usually discouraged extended growth from other flowering shrubs.

**Spanish Superstar** (Ballesteros Grandiflorum): Flamboyant Iberian climber, Spanish Superstar takes well in most soils but thrives mainly in

Europe. Has been successfully transplanted in America but has recently suffered a bout of over-pruning in that country. Regarded by many as the most exciting plant in the world, Spanish Superstar seems destined to take many more major horticultural prizes in the years to come.

**Thomson Supreme** (Australia Culturus): Noted for its simplicity and ability to cope in all conditions, Thomson Supreme first gained recognition in Britain in the early 1950s and in the space of 12 years won the Royal & Ancient Horticultural Society Gold Medal on five occasions. It was felt that Thomson Supreme would never take to American soil conditions but has recently been successfully transplanted in the States where it is displaying vigorous growth.

**Allissum** (Commentatus Urbanum): Once a main feature plant on British courses, the Allissum died back in the early 1970s only to re-appear in a different guise. Now flourishes in high places where the rarified air has given it a new lease of life as it sets a fine example to other high altitude

"You're getting warmer, mister!"

(1979)

plants by its measured growth. Blossoms freely from April to October when its mellifluous scent fills thousands of homes.

**Wild Crenshaw** (Driver Erraticus): Great things were expected from the Wild Crenshaw when it first appeared in America in the mid- 1970s. But its penchant for taking root in undiscovered parts of the course severely restricted its development. Some experts recommended a cutting back of its overlong stems but this proved unsuccessful and the plant is best left alone.

**Dimpled Spheroid** (Surlynus Compressum): The Dimpled Spheroid is easily the most populous plant on any course in the world. Recommended habitat is on closely mown grass but the Dimpled Spheroid has a will of its own and is frequently found in the most inhospitable spots. Available in packs of three, the Dimpled Spheroid stores well in the winter but tends to run riot in the summer.

**Cleveland Weevil** (Agentae Internationalus): Feeds on richly flowering plants where its presence is reputed to reduce growth by up to 25 per cent. It is now so well-established throughout the world that there is little hope of eliminating it although certain plants, such as Spanish Superstar have proved resistant. Regular spraying with a specially formulated chemical called 'Independence' can be effective.

**Flowering Shank** (Lucy Locket): Dreaded growth which appears without warning with low-growing shoots which veer suddenly to the right. Can be eliminated by extensive course of 'Birchenough', the analytical controller that is also recommended for Hook (Sinister Vulgaris), the late-growing, free-running, left-shooting weed and Slice (Dexter Frondissii), the tall-growing, weak-stemmed weed that plagues courses everywhere.

(1986)

## The "Divot" Superstition

**EVENING STANDARD AND ST JAMES'S GAZETTE**
The same man maintained most heretical opinions about the replacing of divots. He argued that the man who discharges what the legend on the tee-boxes declares to be the duty of every golfer, does positive harm to the course; that a very small percentage of replaced divots grow; that those which do not curl up at the edges, and not only provide an execrable lie for any ball which comes to rest on them, but also prevent the young grass

underneath from coming up. He said that what he called the Divot
Superstition has grown up because the golfer who has played a deadly iron
shot at a critical point in the game wants some immediate employment to
prevent him exhibiting signs of exhilaration, which would make his
opponent think the successful shot a fluke, and finds it at the expense of the
course.

(1905)

## Moth Hunting While Golfing

Mr Horace Hutchinson makes the extraordinary confession that he goes
butterfly and moth hunting at the same time when he is competing for golf
championships and the like. "Some of the best of my entomological
specimens have been captured in the course of playing the 'Royal and
Ancient Game'; and, I hope," he says, "without any disloyal neglect of its
prior claims. Some of the most interesting things, too, that I have ever seen
in the way of bird-life dramas I have watched as the golf match went along.
Perhaps I should have played golf more efficiently had I given it a more
whole-souled attention – I do not know. But what I think that I do know is
that I should not have got so much fun out of it altogether; and that, after
all, is, in my opinion (though I may be in a minority) one's chief object in
playing the game.

"Two specimens of moths that I happened to want rather badly for my
collection I had the luck to catch in the long grass (which shows that you
never know what your luck will be when you go off the line) at Sandwich in
course of playing one of the Amateur Championship heats the last time that
Sandwich was the scene of that championship. It was the year that Mr
Travis won. I do not remember against whom I was playing, but I do
remember that it had the most extraordinary effect on him. The moths were
sitting, and as I had a small box in my pocket for the special purpose of such
an occasion it did not take me a quarter of a minute to bag the moths (or
box them), but it hurt the feelings of my opponent dreadfully. He did not
think that I could be taking him seriously enough if I could allow my
attention to wander from him in favour of two dingy-coloured moths. The
fact was that he did not realise how seriously I took the moths. But the
incident upset him badly for two or three holes, and very likely it was only
due to that that I won the match.

# GOLF AT THE ZOO!

By HARRY ROUNTREE

**A GOOD MATCH TO LOSE.**

The Bunny : " Let's see !  Lordy !  I've this for the match ! "

## WHEN IN TROUBLE, BAG A MOTH

"I am not at all sure that it would not be a good stroke to play now and then – when you found yourself in a tight place – to take out a pill-box and bag a moth in it. It is an ingenious way, after all, of suggesting to your opponent that you despise him; which is always a good frame of mind to get him into. Presumably you must not take too long over the capture if you are playing in a competition; otherwise your partner might have you up for 'discontinuing play', which by Rule 13 is prohibited, 'for any reason whatever, except such as is satisfactory to the committee.'

" Reduced to Scratch "

"As to what in this regard would be 'satisfactory' to the committee it must all depend. It must depend on whether the committee was sound on the entomological side. Even so, it is to be presumed that it would be a question of degree. No right-minded committee, it is to be supposed, would disqualify a competitor for going off in pursuit of a Camberwell Beauty, let us say; but a Purple Emperor might be a doubtful reason – on the border line. Much might depend, in the latter case, on the locality. On one of the New Forest courses a Purple Emperor certainly could not be considered a valid excuse for 'discontinuing play'; on the Sandwich links he would be enough of an anomaly to excuse anything. But all this, after all, applies only to a scoring competition. Your opponent in a match has no remedy against you for bird-nesting or butterfly hunting – except not to play with you again."

(1906)

# LOVE ON THE LINKS

## The '99 Championship

*Henry Morrow Hyde*

Levi Chase, twice the champion of the Clayton County Golf club, was practising putting in the hall of his bachelor apartment. He was worried; and all men know that worry interferes with the holing of long putts. Until a month ago he had felt sure of winning the loving-cup (which stood on his sideboard) for the third time. That would have made it his. Now he looked at the cup anxiously. The face of old Tommy Morris, in repoussé silver on its side, seemed to leer at him mockingly.

He remembered what Bessie Jordan had said the night after he had won the cup the second time. They were sitting together on the wide veranda of the club-house on the top of the hill. It was moonlight, and down below them, a mile away, the yellow lights of the town twinkled like stars. He had asked her for the twentieth time to marry him. She had laughed, walked out to the edge of the veranda, stood there for a moment, with the moonlight shining on her scarlet coat, and said, "Wait till you win the cup for the third time, Levi, then ask me again."

So he had come to feel that both the cup and the girl belonged to him. Now that there was a danger he would lose the championship, and at the same time – he tightened his grip on the patent putter in his hand and struck the ball which was lying on the edge of the rug that did duty as a putting green. The ball overran the hole which he had marked with white chalk in the centre, struck a chair leg, and bounded up and through a window opening into the court. He was just in time to see it crash through the skylight four stories below.

Levi Chase uttered a popular golf expletive, threw his putter in a corner, and sat down in an arm-chair. That had been his bunkered luck ever since young Campbell McLain had come to Clayton. McLain had brought letters from some of Chase's friends in New York, and he himself had put him up at the Clayton County Club. The local papers had printed interviews with him the day after his arrival. Chase remembered reading them. "Mr McLain is a splendid golf player," one paragraph began, "having learned his golf on the mother links at St Andrews, Scotland, where the Ancient and Royal

Game has been played for hundreds of years." Chase recalled distinctly the shock that paragraph gave him. It seemed to him, looking back, that it had been a premonition, for that was only the beginning.

McLain had come to Clayton to manage some properties for an English syndicate. That had thrown him into contact with the Hon. Jabez S. Jordan, father of the beautiful Bessie, and, incidentally, the former president of the Clayton Oil Mills. Mr Jordan had invited the young Scotchman to call at his house. There he had, of course, met Bessie. But was that any reason why he should call two or three times a week? Was that any reason why he should offer to teach Miss Bessie the true Scotch swing and the real St Andrews grip? Had not Bessie been under his (Chase's) instruction for two whole seasons? Because a young Scotchman had happened to learn golf at St Andrews, was that any reason why a girl should drive out to the links with him nearly every day, and allow him to hold her hands while he showed her the proper way to grip her clubs?

"SLOWEST FOURSOME IT'S EVER BEEN MY GOOD FORTUNE
TO FOLLOW . . .!!"

It had been maddening, not to say utterly destructive to good golf. Once, looking back from the Duffer's Lament hole to the water-hazard behind the clubhouse, Chase had seen a sudden gleam of white across the back of Bess Jordan's scarlet coat. He could have sworn that McLain was putting his arm around her. That evening, after tea at the club house, he had ventured to remonstrate with her.

"Levi Chase," she had answered, "I should be insulted if I did not know you so well. Mr McLain is teaching me to play golf as they play it at St Andrews. You ought to be enough of a golf-player to appreciate what a privilege that it. When you saw us this afternoon he was showing me how to swing my iron for a lofter-shot over the water hazard."

Then she had walked away, with her cheeks as red as her coat. After that it seemed to Chase that she took particular pains to show him that she was interested in McLain in other than a golf sense, and that as for him he was hopelessly bunkered.

"Damn it!" said Levi Chase, wickedly, "I wish the whole thing was settled!" Then he drank a Scotch-and-soda and went to bed.

Levi Chase was one of your consistent men, both as golf-player and lover. He swung his niblick with a studious air, and he paid court to the fair Lady of the Links in the same serious fashion. Campbell McLain, on the other hand, had an easy and graceful way about him, both with golf-sticks and women. He made phenomenal progress in the affections of Miss Jordan.

"Too bad," said the Club Grandfather to the Green Captain, "that poor old Levi should lose both the Championship and the girl. And hanged if I know which he feels the most cut up about!" Which was a great concession for a true lover of the ancient game.

For a week before the annual tournament opened, Levi lived at the club. While a dew was still on the putting greens he was out practising long putts and getting used to his new Scotch clubs. It was a desperate matter with him. Much more than the Championship depended on his sureness of stroke and he knew it. Almost every day, as he started out on his second afternoon round, he could look back to the clubhouse and see his rival drive up in Miss Jordan's cart. A couple of hours spent in teaching his pretty pupil was all the practice McLain seemed to think she needed. Chase could see them hole out at the Duffer's Lament and tee off for the Lover's Delight. Then they passed out of sight and under the shoulder of a hill. He was always glad when they were gone. The sight was distracting. Once he even caught himself at the top of a swing with his eye off the ball and gazing unmistakably in the direction of Miss Jordan's red coat. To a golfer no sin could be worse. He felt that he was losing his nerve, and with it all hope of Championship form.

On Tuesday morning, the opening day of the tournament, Chase took a long nap. He had drawn with one of the causal twice-a-week-players, and knew that he had an easy thing. When he came downstairs at eleven o'clock the clubhouse and the verandahs were full. It was like a congregation of scarlet-coated flamingoes. McLain had already started on the second round of the nine-hole course. He could see him half-way across the links, and in the little knot of spectators he could make out one figure which he knew was Bess Jordan. His heart was heavy, and his pet driver felt like a baseball bat in his hands.

At any rate, he thought, he was sure of winning his first match and the day of his humiliation was at least forty-eight hours off. He went the rounds listlessly, finishing with only 3 up against a very indifferent player. When he got back, McLain, who had of course beaten his man easily, was sitting on the veranda with Miss Jordan. His air of proprietorship was maddening. Chase felt as though he had foozled a six inch putt at the home hole.

He hardly got a chance to say a word to Bess Jordan that night. She was busy telling some friends, who had driven out to the club for dinner, in what hollow style McLain had beaten his opponent of the morning.

Next day it was harder golf, and when the sun set only McLain and Chase were left, as everybody expected would be the case.

The clubhouse was filled with a gay crowd that evening, but Chase would have none of it. He was determined to die game at least. If he must lose the cup as well as the girl it would only be after a hard fight. Just before going to bed he went out on the verandah to get a breath of fresh air. Bess Jordan's clear voice sounded through the window beside him.

"You expect to win to-morrow, Mr. McLain?" it said.

"I don't want to be boastful, Miss Bess, but really a St Andrews player has every advantage, you know. Yes, I shall win the cup, and if you want to make me very happy you will let me give it to you. I shall always be ready to defend it, and with your inspiration to aid me I shall never lose."

"That would be delightful, Mr McLain," the girl's voice answered. "Quite like the days of chivalry to have a knight always ready to draw his trusty golf stick from its caddie bag. Of course I should like to have the cup."

That was adding insult to injury. Levi Chase walked across the verandah and went up to bed. As he passed Bess Jordan glanced up and saw him.

The great match was not called until eleven o'clock the next morning, to give late sleepers time to get out from the city. McLain won the honour, and led off with a beautiful drive over two hundred yards. His ball fell fair on the green. Chase sliced his drive, as he knew he should do, and fell in the bunker. "The Championship Prize," as the club wit had nicknamed Miss Jordan, early showed the drift of her sympathies. She went on with the little crowd which followed McLain, and left Chase to try his mashie shot with no help from her blue eyes.

McLain won the first hole in four to go with 1 up, and Chase heard Miss Jordan give a little sigh of delight, which he thought very unfeeling of her, to say the least. The next hole was halved, Chase's steadier work with the iron overcoming the advantage of McLain's long drives. On the first round, in fact, Chase was 2 up, and he thought he saw the shadow of a frown on Bess Jordan's face. That, he felt, settled his fate.

McLain finished the second round with 2 up, and the score was halved. The clubhouse was deserted now. Even the club chaperon had left her big easy-chair on the side of the veranda and come out on the links to watch the great game. Both men were playing hair-raising golf.

When they teed off for the thirty-sixth and last hole the Scotchman was 1 up, and was counted a sure winner. McLain had the honour, and just as he raised his club to drive, Chase heard Bess Jordan say something to her father, who stood in the crowd close behind him. Whatever it was it seemed to disconcert the player. He topped his drive and landed in the

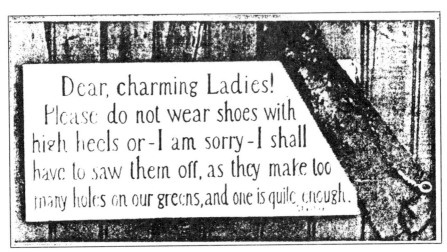

(1927)

ditch not more than fifty yards away. Chase's drive was well placed, but a little short. His brassie shot landed him on the green within a foot of the hole. McLain, playing from a cuppy lie, struck the bunker. It would take him at least two strokes to hole out. The championship and the loving-cup seemed fairly within Levi Chase's grasp, yet strangely he felt a thrill of disappointment, rather than exultation, run over him. He glanced at Bess Jordan. Her face was flushed, and he fancied he could see a trace of tears in her eyes. She was mourning at the coming defeat of McLain.

The gallery was still and expectant. It was gathering in its breath for the cheer that was to greet the victor. Then a strange thing happened:

_Levi Chase overputted the hole by six feet._

McLain played five strokes, and halved the hole with Chase. The Championship and the loving-cup were his.

After dinner Levi Chase sat down in his old seat on the verandah to think it over. As a golfer he had a heavy weight on his conscience. As a lover he felt that he had done right. Just as his mind was getting badly mixed Bess Jordan came round the corner of the clubhouse.

"Levi Chase," she began.

"Well, Miss Jordan?" – with great dignity.

"Make room for me on that bench, if you please. I have come out here to say, sir, that, if you still want me, I am ready to marry you. I saw you last night," she went on, before he could recover his breath, "I saw you go by the window, and I know you heard that idiot McLain promise to give me your loving-cup."

"But I thought you loved him."

"So did I, Levi, until you started to play that last hole, with Mr McLain 1 up. Then all in a moment I knew it was only as a golf-player I loved him, for I fairly ached to have you win. I said so to papa, and Mr McLain heard me. It startled him so that he topped his drive. That gave you a chance to win, but you deliberately missed that last putt because you thought I would be disappointed. That settled it. 'Bess Jordan,' I said to myself, 'when a Champion golfer-player deliberately loses the Championship by missing a six-inch putt in order to spare a girl's feelings, he has given the strongest proof of devotion within the power of man.'"

When they were married a big box came from Campbell McLain. Inside was the loving-cup and a note.

"I promised it to Miss Jordan," the note read, "but Mrs Chase's husband can defend it better than I."

(1899)

## Golfing Garb

*A new sport corset*

Ladies, particularly golfers, tennis players, motorists, yachtswomen, and all who indulge in these and other sports, will, we are sure, be glad to hear of a new sport corset, specially designed for them. The new model is the perfection of a Sport Corset, gradually evolved by years of study and experience, and will confer a great boon on all enthusiastic sportswomen who wish for ease and who yet owe it to themselves to be elegant.

The Sports Corset is made in a new fabric, specially adapted by its porosity, in white or drab; it has no busks, and no lacing at the back, and is fitted with easily removable, unbreakable, non-rusting steels. The busks are replaced by broad elastic across the fronts and the backs cross over and fasten at the side. The comfort of it, the simplicity of adjustment, are remarkable. No more broken busks, no more ugly steels pushing up and protruding through blouse; and again, the steels can be removed in a couple of minutes and the corset is ready for the wash or cleaner. This corset, though originally worked out to meet the sportswoman's requirement, will appeal to many who have been seeking in vain a really comfortable, well-cut corset. The design has bee registered No. 602187.

The Knitted Corset and Clothing Company have recently wonderfully improved their knitted corsets, the shape of which is ideal, and impossible to excel in knitting. For years this company have manufactured a great variety of boneless corsets, and have now added to their department a new French tricot corset, low in the bust, and deep over hips, fitted with suspenders, which give full support without any pressure, and is without doubt the most perfect model of its kind. This company also has the newest and most up-to-date straight-fronted corset at very moderate prices.

There are some figures which no ready-made corset can fit, and to those of our readers who require their corset making to order, we can with greatest confidence recommend them to place themselves in the hands of this firm, whose made-to-order department is in the hands of skilled expert corse-tières. Write today for their list, it is one of the most interesting and complete of the corset trade. The address is the Knitted Corset and Clothing Co., 118 Mansfield Road, Nottingham.

(1912)

## A Fatal Foursome

_Ethel Armitage Southam_

We had quarrelled – it was the worst – I will not say it was the only quarrel we had had since we were married. And the whole thing arose through that stupid foursome.

In a weak moment I consented, with Jim as my partner, to challenge Eva Howard and her brother for a match of 18 holes. What possessed me I cannot imagine – against any ordinary opponent my playing might easily have passed muster, but Eva, as the fates would have it, just happened to be thoroughly on her game, which had the most disastrous effect upon mine. And what made matters worse, Jim simply raved over her shots.

"Splendid! Miss Howard! Oh, you are far too good for us." Again and again he eulogised her strokes, until I, from beginning with nice steady drives and very fair approaches, gradually went absolutely to pieces, until my share of the game dwindled down to nothing but a series of "slices" and "foozles".

At the same time I don't believe I _knew_ Jim until that luckless foursome. I had often played with him during our engagement, and he had merely laughed when I made a bad shot. Matrimony, alas, had changed all; it was no laughing matter _now_, and when at the 17th hole I missed a putt of scarcely more than 12 inches, he assumed an air of such hopeless resignation, that I could bear it no longer.

"There," I cried, "never again as long as I live will I ever play another foursome," stamping my foot, as if to emphasize my words, regardless alike of opponents and caddies. "I hate and detest the game!"

"And no wonder, my dear," retorted my beloved husband. "You have never played a decent stroke the whole afternoon."

I heard no more. At that moment if anybody had asked me who was the most hateful person in the world, I should most unhesitatingly have answered – Jim. I simply picked up my ball, and deliberately bringing the game to an end, marched defiantly off the green.

It was a tragic scene. However much they fight in private, husbands and wives, I believe, invariably try to present a peaceable if indifferent mien in public, but then, it is not every married couple that is mad enough to attempt to play games – and especially golf – together. Take warning, my friends, and *don't*. You may come off all right, the first or even the second year, but after that, it is distinctly dangerous.

We had a miserably uncongenial drive home that afternoon; I sulked the whole of the five miles, and Jim preserved the most tantalisingly stolid demeanour.

"I shall burn every one of my clubs," I murmured threateningly, when I could bear his silence no longer. "Whatever you say nothing will ever induce me to play again."

Jim shrugged his shoulders.

"Well, of course, if you are going to foozle every stroke whenever you find yourself outdriven by a superior player, I cannot see that the game can be much pleasure to you," he returned in the most unconciliatory tone.

"Wretch," I muttered below my breath. Of course I could see what his object was now. He was tired of playing with his wife. I glared at him murderously; it was all a horrible ruse. He was doing his very best to disgust me with golf, so that there would never be any chance of my thrusting myself upon him in any more foursomes.

Why should the wicked always prosper? There was no doubt he had won his day. Never should I play again! For the future, he might rest assured, he would be in a position to ask anybody he wanted, the fascinating Eva every time he chose.

What a ghastly dinner we had that night. We made a praiseworthy effort to keep up a desultory conversation whilst the servants were in the room, but golf being a taboo subject, we both experienced the greatest difficulty in finding topics. Jim would have been perfectly happy if he might only have held forth upon the strokes he had played during the afternoon. But no, I was obdurate as far as the Royal and Ancient game was concerned. If I was not to *play golf* I was quite resolved on one point, never again would I ever *talk* it. I would listen no more to the stories of his marvellous drives, nor attempt to sympathise with him on the days he happened to be "off". I would make myself absolutely disagreeable.

I do not believe Jim half realised what it all meant. A wife who abhors golf, who looks utterly bored every time the word "tee" or "hazard" is mentioned, must undoubtedly be a terrible curse. Yet this is exactly the kind of wife I intended to be, and I quite revelled in the thoughts of this misery I should inflict upon him.

My feelings underwent a slight revulsion, however, when I saw Jim dashing off some letters immediately after dinner, and beheld a note, which I believe he left simply and solely for my edification, lying prominently on the table, in which he informed the secretary of the golf club his wish to offer a silver bowl as a prize for the ladies, to be competed for the last day of the month.

As I read it, my eyes blazed. Just as I suspected, however, now he was preparing to inundate the club with prizes, now there was no longer any chance of his wife winning them. Never mind, Eva was welcome to them all if she liked. I did not want his silly old bowls, he could offer them every week if he chose.

Nevertheless, my eyes refused to close that night. I lay awake hour after hour in a state of the most abject despair. Only as the time wore on, did I seem to grasp what my future meant. No golf! No matches! No clubs! Who but a genuine lover of the game can possibly imagine the terrible vacuum, the wretchedness of my life henceforth . . . words fail me. Let me draw a veil over my feelings.

At any rate that night settled everything – play golf, I must, whatever pride said to the contrary, and if there was a professional to be found, who could improve my game, that individual must be discovered.

"I am going away for a couple of days," I informed Jim, tersely, at breakfast the next morning.

"Going away," he repeated in evident amazement, "what in the world for?"

"I only want to arrange about – about some lessons," I hastened to explain in some trepidation.

"Lessons?"

For a moment I hesitated – should I explain? A glance at Jim, however, dispelled any such good intention.

"Yes – in wood-carving," I proceeded, boldly unheeding the voice of conscience. "I – I must do something," I added, meeting his eyes unflinchingly, although I had a horrible presentiment that my cheeks were turning a lively crimson. "I only want a hobby, and wood-carving will do as well as anything." Once the die is cast, the first little white lie told, what a host of others follow in its train.

Jim simply thrust his hands into his pockets and regarded me with a withering smile.

"The changeableness of you women," he murmured hopelessly. "Yesterday it was all golf, tomorrow it will be nothing but saws and chisels," involuntarily glancing round at some of his treasured old oak which he evidently dreaded falling into my clutches. "How often shall you want lessons?"

"Two or three times a week, I expect," I answered glibly. "I mean to go in for it thoroughly."

I have broached the subject and overcome the first difficulties successfully at the expense, however, of one nasty little story which weighed me down like the proverbial millstone. Yet there were many more worries to be encountered. The anxiety of finding a good coach within reasonable distance, who would, unknown to Jim, improve my game, the agitation of keeping my destination perfectly secret, and the many tactics I should have to adopt regarding my new and imaginary hobby.

Happily Jim is not at all of an inquiring turn of mind, and it just happened, he had several important competitions on, which absorbed most of his attention. Consequently it had never entered his head to ask to see the result of my labours, although he certainly remarked my carving seemed to be "confoundedly tiring" when I returned rather done up on one or two occasions, and startled me somewhat by enquiring how on earth I managed to get so muddy over it.

Luckily, however, an invitation for some golf in Scotland kept him safely out of the way for nearly ten days, during the latter part of the month, so that happily I was spared a good deal of subterfuge.

The 30th, the very day of his return, happened to be the date arranged for the competition for his prize. I had never been near the links since that fatal foursome, but encouraged by the progress I had made under my new coach, and determined at any cost to get my handicap reduced, if only to "twit" Jim, I felt this was an opportunity which I certainly ought to take advantage of.

If I played badly, and did not return a score, there was no occasion for Jim ever to know anything about me I argued; and if – if fortune _should_ smile upon me – well, I will say no more.

The competition was over, and Jim had returned. He had just arrived with all his luggage and his clubs, apparently in the most cheerful frame of mind.

"Oh, I have had a grand time, never played better in my life," he exclaimed as he followed me out of the hall. "And the carving, how is that progressing? Hullo, the bowl," a look of annoyance cross his face, "what on earth have they sent it up here for. It was to have been played for today."

I gazed fixedly into the fire.

"It _has_ been played for," I answered shortly.

He turned and regarded me questioningly. "Then who is the winner? Have you heard?"

"Yes, I have," I cried, turning upon him suddenly with flashing eyes, "I am – _there!_"

For all answer he seized and wrung my hand.

"Don't jeer," I murmured falteringly, "I knew you would."

"Jeer! Why I congratulate you with all my heart. I had a presentiment that bowl would inspire you. Bravo, my dear girl, you will be the best player yet."

"But you are not a bit astonished," I expostulated. "I threatened I should burn every one of my clubs."

"And so have I; mine have been on the point of being cremated or buried hundreds of times, but once a golfer always a golfer. I knew that carving craze would only last a week."

A week! I shook my head. How little he knew me.

(1901)

## The Caddy

_John Roberts_

"You must find that ball," she said peremptorily, as the small sphere bounded wildly away from under his golf stick into the mysterious hollows of the putting greens.

He leisurely surveyed the depression into which the ball had disappeared; then, in compliance with her mandate, raised his voice in a loud shout.

The fresh breeze took up the call of "I say, boy – come here," and carried it to a forlorn figure perched on the fence rails marking the links line of demarcation.

The boy descended slowly from his point of observation and advanced toward the couple. The man in the brown golf suit came forward to meet him.

"Look here," he said in a low tone, "don't you find that ball inside an hour – do you hear?"

A grin of perfect understanding on the upturned freckled face satisfied his instructor, and a bright coin, covertly transferred, further sealed the compact. He returned to the girl's side visibly relieved.

"Oh," she said, "he'll never find it there. Just hold my stick while I show him where it went."

The girl tripped daintily after the urchin, who was plodding aimlessly in the wrong direction.

He watched the two consulting with a clouded countenance.

"It is no use," he muttered, "I've not the ghost of a chance, and she goes home tomorrow." His lips tightened.

The girl came back with a look of determination in her eyes. The wind, taking liberties with her flying draperies, betrayed two slender ankles.

"He shall come to the point this afternoon." She smiled to herself at the thought of the impending Waterloo and the unconscious Wellington. "It must be a blind surrender on his part, and I capitulate gracefully," she whispered gleefully to the wind.

They seated themselves on a protected knoll, below which the green waves sloped away in grassy undulations.

Her profile was temptingly near, and distracting little tendrils of hair fluttered under her cap.

"Must you really go home tomorrow?" he asked at last. Out of the corner of her eye she saw his face was a trifle paler than usual under its coat of tan.

"Yes; and you – when do you go?"

"Tomorrow afternoon. I suppose this summer has been like a lot of others to you?" He spoke slowly, looking at her deliberately.

"It has been very pleasant," she returned artlessly, becoming suddenly absorbed in the tip of her boot.

"Do you care just a little, dear?"

The girl's lips moved, and the man knew, if he did not hear, that they formed "yes."

The world was a beautiful place just at that moment.

"I wonder where that boy can be; he has been gone an hour."

She said this demurely, as if their future depended on his opportune appearance.

"Boy," she called, "what are you doing?"

"Here I am, marm," and the owner of the unkempt head bobbed up serenely from the other side of the sloping bank.

"I ain't never moved," he said. "That gent there, he gave me one, too." He looked reproachfully at the man.

It was clear he must work out his own defence.

Diving into mysterious trouser pockets he exposed to view two dirty palms, in each of which reposed a shining half-dollar.

"You don't mean," she began to the man. Then their eyes met guiltily – conspirator versus conspirator.

In that moment they read each other's souls.

(1899)

By permission of the "Girls' Own Paper."

**A GOOD SWING.**

(1899)          **From a drawing by Garden G. Smith.**

## A FAIR VICTIM OF GOLF

I fondly hoped, when wooed by Jack,
I'd be his only love.
I little thought he'd worship golf,
And cast me like a glove.

"The mountain would not come to me,"
So _I_ perforce must play;
Alas! my futile efforts showed
I ne'er could be "au fait".

I long to change the dreary links
For gardens sweet with flowers;
But if I dare to hint as much,
My husband only glowers.

(1912)

While others hie to moor or glen,
In search of stag or grouse;
A seaside town's the cruel fate
Of every golfer's spouse.

Oh! how I hate this golfing shop,
The sameness of it all!
"How to decrease your handicap",
Or "get a longer ball".

If you would wed a golfing man,
You'd best take my advice,
Founded on sad experience:
Before you do – think twice.

_W. L. P._

## DRIVING FROM THE TEE

She stood at the address,
With conscious power withal;
Her mind intent upon the stroke,
Her eye fixed on the ball.
Her swing was ease and grace,
And the stroke both firm and free,
That made the ball, like startled bird,
Fly whirring from the tee.

I watched her through the green,
And saw her game was good;
Whether she used an iron club,
Or one that's made of wood.
In drive, approach, and putt,
She shone in all the three.
But ah! the poetry of golf
Was her driving from the tee.

(1898)

Pardon, dear maid! I cried,
While I confess with shame,
That till I saw you play, I thought
No charm lay in the game.
Now pleasure's widest field
Is opened up to me,
When your bewitching, graceful form
Is driving from the tee.

_Ronald Ross_

# THE ALPHABET OF GOLF

*Chris Plumridge*

**A** IS FOR ANGLE
The degree by which a golf ball can be diverted from its intended course.

**B** IS FOR BOTCH
The potential outcome of every golf shot.

**C** IS FOR CUNNING
Particularly of the low animal kind often demonstrated by your opponent at the vital stage of a match.

**D** IS FOR DOG
When you've just played like one be grateful you don't have to go around seeking the nearest lamp post.

**E** IS FOR EINSTEIN
Most backswings defy the theory of relativity by proving that there can be transmission of energy with a velocity greater than that of light. This also proves that Einstein was never a golfer or maybe he just couldn't get into a club.

**F** IS FOR FATE
The mysterious force that assists everyone else bar you.

**G** IS FOR GONE
When you've finished a round of golf you find that the following have gone: several golf balls, the lace on your left shoe, your concentration, your temper, your brain and quite probably your back.

**H** IS FOR HOOK
The eventual outcome of your controlled draw.

**I** IS FOR INSPIRATION
The longer you play, the less you find it.

**J** IS FOR JOKE
I thought my swing was funny until I saw yours.

**K** IS FOR KNOCK
Hollow sound made when a golf ball strikes a tree.

**L** IS FOR LOST
What becomes of your ball when it does strike a tree.

**M** IS FOR MONEY
Coloured paper that you part with at the end of a round.

**N** IS FOR NUMERATE
Many golfers find it difficult to count beyond five.

**O** IS FOR ORIFICE
Aperture on each green that refuses to accommodate your ball.

**P** IS FOR PAR
Figures that appear printed but are rarely copied by hand.

**Q** IS FOR QUIET
Please!

**R** IS FOR ROUND
Yours, I think.

**S** IS FOR SLICE
The eventual outcome of your controlled fade.

**T** IS FOR TROUBLE
Easy to get into, hard to get out of.

**U** IS FOR UNPRINTABLE
Description of language commonly used on golf courses.

**V** IS FOR VACUUM
The space between our ears which becomes entirely void of matter when we set foot on the course.

**W** IS FOR WHACK
(See K for Knock)

**X** IS FOR XANTHIPPE
The wife of Socrates who was noted as an ill-tempered, scolding, shrewish woman. He didn't spend too much time in the bar after a round either.

**Y** IS FOR YOUTH
Where did it go?

**Z** IS FOR ZIGZAG
When did you last hit two straight shots consecutively?

(1986)

# HIGH STAKES

## I Was Robbed

*Graham Cant*

Golf for most of us is rather like the Mad Hatter's Tea Party – cake yesterday, cake tomorrow, but never cake today. We are forced to fondle our memories of past triumphs and our hopes for the future, for today, oddly enough, we are not playing our "usual game". You might suppose that this would become rather depressing, and, indeed I believe cases of acute melancholia are not unknown amongst golfers, but these are probably beginners, for any really experienced player realises that it is not his game that is at fault but some disturbing influence over which he has little if any control. He would have played a splendid round, if . . .

Now, don't let's have any misunderstanding about this "if" business. No golfer would dream of offering an excuse for his bad play, for that would be a most unsportsmanlike thing to do. He may, however, with perfect

(1947)

propriety, offer an alibi, for an alibi, unlike an excuse, is intended for home consumption. If the player himself believes in it, and normally he does with a wholehearted fervour, then it has served its purpose. If it should also convince an opponent or partner, so much the better, but no one should expect too much.

Bad luck should be invoked as sparingly as possible. Once admit its existence and some unkind person is sure to wonder whether that spectacular approach you had at the third was not due to good luck rather than skill. Besides, no golfer should look upon himself as the plaything of blind chance. Rather should he feel like some Homeric figure battling bravely against titanic forces. Luck certainly plays a large part in crude games like tennis and billiards, but has little place in the noble and scientific game of golf.

## ALLEGED HELPERS

Our forefathers relied very heavily upon their caddies to provide the necessary alibi for their bad play. And rightly so, for any recollection of caddie stories reveals that these alleged helpers spent their whole time in uttering derogatory and insulting remarks about their employers, or doing all in their power to put them off their stroke.

Modern golfers, deprived of this staple alibi, often sigh nostalgically for the days that are gone. They really have no cause to, for the caddie-cart has inherited many of the endearing characteristics of its human prototype. For example, is it at hand when you reach the tee? Of course not, that's it 50 yards away right on the other side of the green. And have you never listened to a caddie-cart in the wind? It can whistle every bit as lugubriously as the worst of human bag carriers.

And talk of gratitude! I've seen a man oil his cart's hubs and pump its tyres until it moved at a touch. Left unattended upon what seemed perfectly level ground and in a dead calm, it attacked its owner savagely from the rear, just as the wretched man was dealing with a delicate pitch over a bunker. The human caddie stopped short of actual violence.

Clubs, too, used to figure highly on the alibi list and I cannot understand why the good old custom of breaking them and throwing them away has been allowed to fall into disuse. Are steel shafts supposed to know more about the game than hickories? Is it a question of expense, or fear of injury? Whatever the reason, the links are much duller without the merry whirr of clubs passing overhead.

Greens committees, however, are still with us, providing us with flags in impossible places, unraked bunkers, divot marks on fairways, plugged balls and ladies' foursomes. If greens committees ever started to try to please their members, the game would become intolerable, for we should be deprived of at least 50 per cent of our alibis. Fortunately, this is unlikely ever to happen, for greens committees have for long taken refuge in the dictum "Conditions are the same for everyone." What nonsense! The merest beginner know that it is the scientific player with the grooved swing who is most affected by unnatural conditions. The basher doesn't suffer at all.

I have mentioned some of the more popular alibis. Ingenious golfers will readily think up others for themselves. One man I know can never play good golf on Monday. Another finds the precarious state of his health, particularly on medal days, an ever-present threat to his game.

But perhaps the best alibis, and the ones most readily believed by others, are met with in extreme youth. A few years ago a young man, after losing in the first round of the Boys' Championship, was heard to explain to his father: "Daddy, how could I win? That boy had a caddie cart and – a LEFT-HAND GLOVE."

(1959)

## Skins, Strings, Scrambles, Specks, and No Alibis

*David Davies*

Jack Nicklaus, in that "skins" game in Scottsdale, Arizona earlier this year, holed a putt worth 240,000 dollars, about 30,000 dollars per foot as it happened, and very commendable too.

Even for one of the relatively few men to have made real millions out of golf, putting for that kind of money still represented real pressure for Nicklaus, and the fact that he threw his putter high in the air, he knew not where, showed that it meant something to him. But not as much as a three-foot putt once meant to me in the humbler, but infinitely more homely, surroundings of Aberystwyth golf club, in that blessed part of Wales where there is still real beer and songs are properly sung.

Like Nicklaus, and come to that Tom Watson, Gary Player and Arnold Palmer, we were playing a variation of the normal form of the game. In the case of the luminaries, they were playing a format that demanded an

THE MISSED PUTT.

The grand old Spirit of the Foursome—from the point of view of the Man who is
off his Game.

(1912)

outright win at a hole to take the money; we were playing an ordinary fourball, except that the stakes were slightly unusual. Whereas Nicklaus and company were playing for a total of 360,000 dollars, we were playing for an hour's free drinking. That was the basic bet.

There were bags of roasted peanuts on oozlers, pork scratchings for birdies and I have to tell you that my partner and I managed to win. In fact we won in the morning and again in the afternoon, whereupon the realisation dawned that we were in for two hours' free drinking that night in the Prince Albert, draught Bass and all.

Now if there is one thing worse than an hour's free drinking in that company, it is two hours', which is where the three footer comes in. We had negotiated an extra hour on the bye in the afternoon and by serious mismanagement my partner had that three-footer on the 18th to win that bet as well. I do not say that he took any notice of me on my bended knees, imploring him to miss, but miss he did, and the one back, and we were saved.

**DRINKING BETER THAN CASH**

I suppose even the greediest of us, drinking, say, Campari for an hour, would be pushed to get through much more than £7–8, so the money is not a factor. But playing that form of the game adds so much to the round that it has become a part of our golfing lives.

It is far preferable to vulgar cash, and to avoid that we have played for things like who drives the four-ball to Royal Dornoch and even for who sits next to our ace non-flier on the trip to Spain. He is a man so constitutionally incapable of sitting soberly in an aircraft seat that he causes dementia in air stewardesses, often before take-off.

But the point is that the ordinary fourball, played week in and week out by most of us, can be livened up and I feel it is a pity that our club committee do not encourage us more in this. Late last year I played in a Scramble, a fascinating and extremely friendly form of the game in which four players partner each other. All four drive, the best drive is selected and all four play a shot from that point.

The best result of that is selected and all four . . . and so on. In our match one of our team, at the last hole, played three superb shots to a par five and we used his effort every time. I then holed a four-foot birdie putt and was never more pleased with myself.

(1957)

## THE NO-ALIBI TOURNAMENT

Then there is what the Americans call the No Alibi tournament. Instead of deducting your handicap at the end of the round you are allowed to replay, during the round, the number of shots equalling three-quarters of your handicap. It applies equally on or through the green with the catch that a stroke replayed *must* be used, even if it is worse than the original, that it cannot be replayed a second time.

A few clubs I know have tried the String tournament. This is where you give each competitor a piece of string measuring a foot for each handicap stroke. He can then use as much or as little of it as he likes to move his ball from nasty places, cutting off as much as he needs at the time. You can then use it to hole a putt.

The problem is in getting the right proportions of string to ability. A good player of say two handicap can do miracles with an allowance of two feet, while 20 yards might not help some of us after a really wild one.

You may well have heard of the late Walter Hagen's maxim, trotted out after he had holed yet another outrageous putt, that "three of them and one of those always equals four". That, of course, hardly makes it the less infuriating when you are on the receiving end, which makes the Speck system one worth considering.

This can be adapted to ordinary fourball match play, and each team gets a speck, or point, for (a) the longest drive in the fairway, (b) for getting the first ball on the green, (c) for having the closest ball to the pin on the approach shot, (d) for a one-putt green and (e) for the lowest score on the hole. It would then be possible to halve a hole and still win it by three specks to one and get some satisfaction for superior striking.

There are dozens of other variations, most of them worth a try. They may be flirtations from what we properly regard as the most satisfying way of playing, but they can be fun. Remember to leave some time for the free drinking afterwards.

(1985)

(1961)

# TRAVELLERS' TALES

## On Holiday

*Henry Longhurst*

Half the fun of holidays lies in the anticipation and in this sense it is a great pleasure to me to set down some of my thoughts on golfing holidays because, although I like to think it is a subject on which I am really rather knowledgeable, I cannot remember when I last took one myself. Indeed I cannot remember when I last took a holiday at all in the recognised sense of the term, namely being totally free from thought of one's daily bread. So many people refer to my way of life as "one long holiday" that I have almost come to believe it myself, but you can never be really "on holiday" if there is an article due on Sunday and/or Monday and/or Tuesday, and in some weeks on all three. However, enough about my own curious problems. I am now going to take a golfing holiday on paper.

For this congenial purpose I assemble three friends and a good-sized motor car, preferably belonging to one of them who does not like anyone to drive it but himself, or at any rate does not want me to drive it. It will be noted that there is no room for wives in the vehicle. As a reluctant concession I would permit wives and two motor cars, so long as none of the former played golf. (No, no. On second thoughts I wouldn't!)

My friends would be known well to each other, though not all from the same part of the world, and they would have played golf with each other on many occasions in the past but not frequently enough to have become staled with each other's golf or company. There would be among us a strong competitive "edge", based possibly on past matches, or Yorkshire v. the pampered South, or some such. Our handicaps and general form would be known to each other but that does not say that tomorrow's match would not be subject to overnight haggling.

Assuming for the moment that we are not going abroad, I should have the owner of the car make arrangements for it, and us, to be conveyed overnight by train to Scotland. There is something indefinable about golf in Scotland that gives it a flavour superior, to the connoisseur, to golf in any other part of the world, though that is a point which I have not space to enlarge upon now. Incidentally, and a most important point, the owner of

the car would be appointed treasurer for the whole period. He would settle the fare for the car and sleepers; he would pay the porters; he would pay the hotel bills, green fees, petrol and all incidental expenditure which was common to the party. At the end, without rendering any form of account, he would say, "I want a cheque for £x from each of you."

## UNANIMOUS DESIRE

Throughout our trip we should play foursomes after lunch and singles or three-balls in the morning. There would not be any argument about this because it would be the unanimous desire of the company. The three-balls would enable anyone who did not particularly want to play at that moment to sit out, as it were, as "dummy". The three-ball to my mind is in any case one of the very best forms of golf because, whereas in a four-ball half your shots don't count at all, in a three-ball they all count double. There would, however, be one outstanding exception, and rather a strange one at that. If our travels did not allow us a lot of time at St Andrews, we should play a four-ball round the Old Course because the interest of actually playing the Old Course exceeds that of any match that one may make upon it and everybody would therefore want their own chance of setting their wits and skill against that greatest of all opponents.

We should then – it being August or, better still, September – proceed northwards, taking in a day at Nairn and then a day at Dornoch. I have not been there since before the war and I understand they have "modernised" the course, which sounds ominous, but nothing that man could do could modernise the wonderful sense of tranquillity and remoteness that prevails when you get that far from what we in England are pleased to call civilisation. They did not even have keys to the hotel bedrooms, I remember. Nobody ever seemed to want them, they said.

## PLAYED IN DINNER JACKETS

Up to this time I should have been adopting towards the party that faintly superior air of the fellow who has "been here before". From Dornoch onwards we should be pioneers together. Our next stop would be Cruden Bay, which everyone tells me is wonderful and which remains a sad gap in my own golfing education. It would, I imagine, be light until nearly midnight and something tells me that at some point a challenge match would arise, to be played in dinner jackets.

We should then forget about the golf for a while and make our way down in leisurely style along that staggeringly beautiful road that crosses Scotland diagonally from right to left and takes in Loch Ness and Glencoe. Then, leaving the car in Glasgow, we should fly first to Campbelltown for a game at Macrihanish and thence to the Isle of Islay to stay at Machrie with mine host who wears a kilt, hails from Blackpool, is county councillor for an area half the size of England and has four beautiful daughters. Here is the perfect natural golf, left to look after itself in the winter while the greenkeeper goes off trapping rabbits.

There are also on the island several distilleries, to at least one of which I should have secured an introduction for the party before we left.

Perhaps when we got back to Glasgow there would be time for a few days at Turnberry Hotel, playing the lovely course there and making a pilgrimage or two to Prestwick, Troon and Western Gailes. If not, what a splendid excuse to come back next year and start all over again. After all, we have missed out Edinburgh completely. What about North Berwick, Muirfield, Gullane and Luffness? Hang it, I have almost talked myself into taking a holiday myself!

(1957)

## Force Eight

*Michael Williams*

**Sometime in August:** The lighthouseman at Trevose Head put up what seemed to be a very solid case. He simply could not understand why so many people flew off to Spain for their summer holidays.

After all, he argued with all the vehemence of someone who had actually tried it, it is shoulder to shoulder on beaches not exactly renowned for their cleanliness, so much sun that you spend most of the night daubing yourself with some cooling lotion, suffering water you cannot drink and spending at least one day within sprinting range of a loo that, in all probability, will not work.

There was nothing, he surmised, like England or, to be more exact since he was a Cornishman, Cornwall. As the sun dappled on Constantine Bay and the sea surged gently round the headland to Padstow and, beyond, Polzeath, one had to agree. There was also, on the morrow, the prospect of golf, a foursomes competition under the banner of the adjacently based 42nd RAF Torpedo Squadron at St Mawgan.

The morrow threw a rather different slant. On turning the corner of the Trevose clubhouse en route for the first tee, the umbrella was promptly turned inside out and a hasty retreat beaten while waterproofs were donned as protection against rain that was not so much coming down as hurtling horizontally.

## RAINDROPS EXPLODING ON THE FACE

It also stung, like hail, not because it was hail but because it was travelling so fast on the wind that the raindrops exploded on the face. Peter, the RAF chappie who was one of our companions, said quite cheerfully: "Force eight, gusting force nine".

Roger, his partner, seemed oblivious. As he lived in these parts, the thought occurred that the weather was by no means out of the ordinary. In fact, he had imbibed rather too freely the night before and was suffering from a distinctly sore head. At least he could have imagined himself to be standing under a cold shower, albeit in his waterproofs.

If it was no day for golf, it was certainly not a day for the 32-handicap chief cook, bottle washer, housekeeper, gardener, medic, advisor on homework, organiser of picnics, furniture restorer, mechanic, provider of clean clothes, otherwise known as the lady wife, to make her début in what could loosely be called open competition.

She had not been exactly smitten with the idea in the first place, less so when she learned as we cowered in the lee of the starter's hut that Roger had recently set a new course record.

We got a five at the first to their six and when they left three shots in a bunker at the second, she began to appreciate that even the better players are human after all.

As the wind increased in force and the rain found its way beyond the most waterproof of waterproofs (according to the manufacturers) there was talk of packing it all in after nine holes. It seemed a rattling good idea.

But at that moment the lady wife holed another putt, next stuffed another mis-hit chip close to the flag and the mathematics on a now-sodden card revealed that we had somehow accumulated enough points to be obliged to keep going. Peter and Roger were very good about it.

Remarkably, if not miraculously, we even got into "the frame" but the lady wife was so weather-beaten that she came off the 18th green like a dazed marathon runner, her mind fixed only on a hot bath and a bed on which she remained recumbent for the rest of the day.

I, having once played at Ballybunion, was more acclimatised to such days and retired to the bar at which, using the description of another first-time visitor to Trevose, "80 people appeared to be standing up and all shouting at one another."

A little thing like a drop of rain and a good blow off the Atlantic was all part of Trevose, with Peter Gammon, who owns the place, insisting on foursomes and singles only and a speed of play that would frighten the life out of half of today's golfers.

It is the sort of place where a playwright like Alan Bennett would have a feast. It may also explain why so many have been coming back for so long.

(1985)

## Golf in Excelsis

Under this title *Mr Punch* makes most excellent fun of the visit of the four British professionals to Mexico. "In view," our contemporary says, "of the exceptional political importance of the visit of the four famous British golfers to Mexico, *Mr Punch* has arranged with Mr Raymond Blatherwick, the famous interviewer, who accompanies the party, to send a series of letters for exclusive use in these columns." The first instalment arrived yesterday, and ran as follows:

**New York, January 1st** We arrived today, after a somewhat stormy voyage, but it is satisfactory to relate that the illustrious quartet are all in excellent fettle for their Mexican campaign. The serious spirit in which they undertook to prepare themselves for the fray was apparent from the outset. Jack White, a man of studious tastes, spent most of his time studying Spanish, with a view, as he owned, of being able to converse with President Porfirio Diaz in his native tongue.

Andrew Kirkaldy, who is noted for his strong theological bias, had provided himself with several works on the Aztec race, and was much impressed by the theory which identifies them with the Lost Tribes, and often engaged in heated controversies with his fellow Scot, Alexander Herd. Rowland Jones, a Welshman, and an ardent politician, was intensely interested in the speeches of Mr Lloyd-George, as they were reported from time to time by wireless telegraphy. But exercise and training were not

GOLF IN OLD JAPAN.—NO. 2.  THE DRIVE.

neglected. By an arrangement with the chief engineer, the champions were able to get an hour's niblick play in the coal bunkers every morning, and Andrew Kirkaldy had the satisfaction of driving over a passing iceberg from the hurricane deck. In the evenings the quartet sang part songs or practised putting in the saloon. Rowland Jones occasionally improvised some sparkling penillions, and Jack White accompanied him on the castanets. In the early stages of the voyage Andrew Kirkaldy's appetite suffered from the motion of the liner, but his spirits were happily unimpaired, and his table talk was enriched by many brilliant *bons mots*. Thus, on nearing America, he asked, "Why was Jack White?" and, pointing to Sandy Herd, immediately answered, "Because he saw Sandy Hook."

This remarkable impromptu was at once marconigraphed to the White House, and caused a distinct slump in Mexican securities on Wall Street.

**Washington, January 3rd** I have just seen Rowland Jones, who tells me that the breakfast with the President was a great success. The only other guests besides the golfing champions were Elihu Root and Booker Washington, and it appears that a slight awkwardness was caused when Andrew Kirkaldy, who sat next to Mr Washington, asked him whether he thought that any American football team could hold their own against the "All Blacks", a question which his neighbour interpreted as bearing on the negro problem. However, Mr Roosevelt intervened with his usual breezy energy, and diverted the conversation to the influence of golf on the popularity of statesmen, the proper pronunciation of the word Schenectady, the superiority of buckwheat cakes to Scotch scones, and the claims of Mr Andrew Lang to be regarded as a serious historian.

Andrew Kirkaldy, who, as a neighbour of Mr Lang's, held decided views on this subject, said that when the Japanese took to golf they would be "just a classical people". Jack White thought that the White House compared unfavourably with the Golf Club House at Sunningdale, but he liked the President's affability. "Not the build for a scratch player," he added, "but I dare say he would soon play as well as the Duke of Devonshire or Mr James Bryce." Sandy Herd made great friends with Mr Root, whom he enlightened on the Scottish Church question, and after breakfast the President instructed his guests in the use of the lasso, which he warned them might be needful in some of the Mexican back blocks.

**Chihuahua, January 7th** We came on here this morning by special train, with outriders, after a short visit to the President at Mexico City. Don Porfirio was kindness itself, and insisted on changing hats, according

to an old Castilian custom, with Jack White as they parted on the doorstep. The heat is something terrific, but we all wear sombreros with refrigerators and white Nainsook trousers. On our arrival we were met at the station by a deputation of Toltecs, accompanied by the Chapultepec band, playing on zumpangos, mulucs, cauacs, and other Aztec instruments. After a hurried lunch at the hotel, we proceeded to the links, where a large crowd was awaiting our arrival.

Four singles had been arranged in which the British contingent were opposed by local professionals, but I regret to say that on this occasion none of the former showed their true form. For this untoward result, however, the peculiar conditions of the game readily accounted. To begin with, the caddies are mounted on mustangs, which proved so disconcerting that Rowland Jones, a man of highly-strung Celtic temperament, invariably missed his tee shot. Andrew Kirkaldy's opponent was a sinister-looking mesocephalic Aztec named Mictlanteuctli, whose name alone, as Andrew put it, was as bad as giving a stroke a hole, while Jack White was equally paralysed by his association with a Toltec brave, whose patronymic was Ixtlilxochitl. Sandy Herd was the best off, as he was matched with a Mexican Inca named Ramon Guttierez, who, strangely enough, preferred using a rubber-cored ball.

At every second tee refreshments were served, consisting of *octli* or Aztec beer and hot banana fritters, and further delay was caused by Jack White's opponent, who insisted on bathing in a small pond which formed the chief hazard of the thirteenth hole. Guttierez, the Inca mentioned above, surpassed himself by his *bunca* play, but as a rule the local men scored more by the failure of their opponents than by their own brilliance. There is talk, however, of a human sacrifice in our honour tonight, and tomorrow morning we move on to Jalapa, where an exhibition match will be played for the benefit of the amateurs of the Tezcatlipoca golf club.

(1906)

## Golf on a Liner

*From J. S. S.*

A serious student of golf may say that to bring it into the category of ships' games, which are usually of a very bumble-puppy order, is a frivolity to be sternly reproved, but a few hints may be of interest to those of more unorthodox taste who care to hear of a new diversion for the occasionally tedious hours of an ocean voyage.

Given a complacent commander, a handy quarter-deck man, a not too crowded ship, a fairly long promenade deck, and a body of passengers not too insistent on their rights of tenure, the game is easily arranged.

The clubs are composed of a shaft about 2 feet 6 inches long let at an angle into a flat board about 6 inches by 4 inches. The head should be firmly fixed, as it becomes a dangerous missile if it gets loose. The club can of course be used either right- or left-handed. The length and number of holes depend on limitations of space. The ball is a "grummet", a spliced rope ring about four inches' outside diameter. The holes are rings chalked on the deck, placed so as to put a premium on accurate approaching, for instance, in an alley way between the deckhouses, so that the hole has to be played round a corner, as shown in the "Ginger-beer" hole, where the chalk lines can be made out in the sunlight.

Some obvious local rules have to be introduced to deal with scuppers and other hazards, and stymie conditions in or within a few inches of the hole.

It must be admitted that human bunkers are a difficulty if inclined to be disobliging, and to insist on their rights to the deck. We are unfortunately used to associating bunkers with strong expressions, as instanced in the well-known tale, but a new phase is introduced when the bunker itself (or rather himself, we must absolve the gentler sex from all suspicion of unladylike phraseology) begins to say things. The seafaring golfer may get much amusement out of this kind of deck golf.

(1906)

## Golf at Lisbon

You can get golf all over the world nowadays, but a description of a new golf course established upon the ground of the Lisbon Cricket Club at Cruz Quebrada, and forwarded to me (says the golf editor of the _Birmingham Daily Mail_) by a friend out there, does not sound very tempting. From the nature of the communication, I can only extract a few details of this extraordinary course.

"It is," writes my friend, who has a mind for a merry jest, "in the form of a four-sided square with the centre in the middle. It is six miles from the nearest reliable public-house in Lisbon, and can easily be reached by road, rail, sea, or balloon. Attention must be called to the space marked 'Danger Zone' on the map accompanying. It will readily be seen from hole No. 1 to No. 2 (and consequently also from hole No. 5 to hole No. 6), and from hole No. 3 to No. 4, all play across this space at different angles. There is an English cemetery at Lisbon, and a few small burying grounds in the neighbourhood. In spite of these conveniences, I propose to meet this objection by the introduction of my patent bomb-proof shelters for pale people, for which I confidently anticipate a large demand.

"Turning to the question of caddies, I may remark that these are to be obtained in abundance. In manners and customs they may be described as offensive. When engaged to caddy, however, they exhibit many lovable traits, among them being the habit of continually striking (preferably with a wooden club) any loose objects, such as rocks, and an apparently incurable fondness for debate upon the putting greens. As, however, they have a weakness for standing within the driver's swing, it is probable that the tribe will shortly become extinct. Owing to the nature of the ground, it has not yet been possible to replace any divots, as it would not be possible to cut one except with a chisel. At the present time there are about ten persons who make use of the links, and should you contemplate visiting the course, I shall be happy to furnish you with all further information." From which it may be assumed that however good the climate may be, Lisbon is no place for a golfing holiday.

(1906))

(1961)    **"I'M ITCHING FOR A DAMN GOOD DRIVE"**

## Local Rules at Sea

Golf, we know, is played the wide world over, but I never knew before the other day (says a writer in the _Birmingham Daily Mail_) that the game could be played on the high seas. Yet, where there's a will there's a way, it seems. A correspondent sends me a copy of the rules of the RMS _Tarquah_ Golf Club. The rules of St Andrews are adopted _en bloc_, subject only to such local rules as the committee may consider necessary to meet the requirements of the case. It is from the local rules that one can gather what sort of a game golf is when played at sea, and I therefore give you a few of these:

1. No person shall be allowed to play unless he holds a member's card, and has paid for the same.
2. The proceeds of the sale of members' cards shall be given to the Liverpool Seamen's Orphanage.
3. A ball driven off the course may be replaced at a distance of one foot. Penalty one stroke.
4. A ball driven in the bunker (i.e. scupper) may be replaced on deck at a distance of one foot. Penalty one stroke.
5. A ball driven overboard is considered "lost". Penalty two strokes and 1s. to the Orphanage, and 6d. for a new ball.
6. A ball driven into the coal bunker wins the game.
7. Members are requested to replace the turf.
8. Members are advised not to jump after the balls driven overboard.
9. Caddies may be selected from the committee at a nominal rate of 15s. 9d. per round of nine holes.

There is much virtue in that advisory note which passes as rule eight, but I fear me the nautical golfer will greatly miss the pleasure of the big drive.
(1906)

## Tropical Golf

_John Fawcus_

I play on a municipal golf course which is, I am told, positively the dullest in Britain. No tears, no fuss, it's as flat as a pancake and has no tricky bits. But that's the way I like it – after golf in the tropics.

The golf bug really bit me in my first Burma campaign when our gun site was on Maungdaw island, in the Arakan. We were surrounded by a river, a swamp, and the Japanese, all of which tended to keep us within the perimeter.

Because of this the golf craze spread like wildfire when a new bod produced a putter and an ancient ball. I was amazed to find the number of shots which can be made with just a putter.

On the first day only two people knew how to play golf at all, but on the second there were 116 enthusiastic experts, including the sweeper-upper.

True, a foursome using the one ball used to take hours to negotiate the nine holes we laid out in the paddy, but it was better than the eternal cribbage. Also the putter was a great favourite for killing sunbathing snakes, and "take posts" were frequent.

We lost the ball after two months when a monkey ran away with it – and back we went to cribbage.

My next experience of tropical golf came while I was on leave in the mountains near Darjeeling, where a tea-planter friend had made his own small course. It did at least have greens, which was more than the unit's had.

There were several snags, however, all of them Himalayan bears! It was a rule of the course that you must run uphill if chased by one of them. Going downhill was rated as pretty effective suicide because the brown bear turns himself into a ball and rolls down faster than you can run.

I still maintain that rustlings of twigs were made by my friend to make me muff shots!

There was one course that even I did not fancy, somehow. It was at Singapore and was flanked by a jail, a lunatic asylum, a graveyard, a hospital and a maternity home.

## FORGET NOT THE HIPPOPOTAMUS

The place with the craziest local rule is surely Jinja, Uganda, where you remove your ball from the footprint of a hippo without penalty.

Hippos used to come from the nearby lake at night to graze, and you were strongly advised not to walk between them and the lake shore because one man had been killed this way on the fifth or sixth hole.

I think the most glamorous 19th hole in the world is at Nairobi, where a nearby hotel is used as a clubhouse. The equator is claimed to run through the bar and a line has been put on the floor so that you can have a drink with a foot in each hemisphere.

At Mwanza, Tanganyika, your caddy will probably carry a gun to fire in the air if a lion decides to join in the game. It shouldn't put you off because it usually scares them away. At least, I've never met anyone who was there when it failed!

There is one course where I don't advise you to take on the locals for a cash stake – Guayaquil in Ecuador. There they got so fed-up with flooding that they had their greens made of cement, slightly inclined. I don't need to say what happens with a normal approach shot!

It is Bolivia that claims to have the highest course in the world. It is at La Paz, 13,500 feet up. At that height you can just about swing your club unaided, you always seem out of breath and it's darned cold.

I've always wanted to play golf in France, on one of those Riviera courses where a luscious young woman acts as caddy for you. But I expect I'd muff my approach shots, so I guess I'm better off on that flat old municipal course!

(1951)


## Golf on the Riviera

_P. A. Ward-Thomas_

It had been a long summer, exciting, memorable and not a little tiring, so when it was done we went to the south of France in search of contrast, a rest from golf and above all a last few days in the sun before facing the Stygian horror which is winter in Manchester.

Two beautiful weeks passed and then one day we came to Cagnes. As we climbed the precipitous winding lane to the old fortified town high above the green, sweet-smelling valleys and the unbelievable sea the sense of escape was complete. With every stride the decades fell away and the centuries with them for the ancient beauty of this timeless place has changed but little since its inhabitants defied the invading Saracens 700 years ago.

In the still air and cool silence of the tiny narrow streets it was almost impossible to believe that the twentieth century was only ten minutes' walk away. Thoughts of Renoir, Matisse, Soutine and other great painters who had lived in Cagnes came easily to mind; some of the world's great chefs, amongst them Escoffier and Aubin were born in the little town too, but one never expected to find golfers.

There could be few places which seem more remote from the game and yet how wrong we proved to be. When by accident the word golf was mentioned at dinner that night, our host and friend, M. Vuffray, who knows so well the strange intimacy of life in Cagnes, told us that within a few yards of his house lived the most distinguished of France's *professeurs du golf*, Auguste Boyer, and one of her best present-day players, Albert Pelissier, who appears quite often in the British tournaments.

Pelissier I knew, but was anxious to meet Boyer, of whom I had heard much, and the next evening found us in one of those deceptive houses which one often encounters in France – quiet and simple outside, tranquil and charming within. We had not been there more than a few minutes when M. Bardana, whom I had watched reach the last eight at Worplesdon three weeks before, arrived. Bardana, who won the French championship from the inevitable Lamaze last year, runs a restaurant on the coast and in his spare time hits a golf ball remarkably well. Thus, then, the illusion that I could escape from golf was dispelled, but how charmingly it was done in the ebb and flow of reminiscence.

In the years between the wars Boyer and his great contemporaries, Aubrey Boomer and Marcel Dallemagne, were the outstanding European professionals and were winning the championships of Germany, Italy, France and Belgium when Cotton and Percy Alliss were at their finest and used to compete regularly. Boyer now has what seemed to us an idyllic existence for a professional. His summer is divided between Italy and Switzerland, and then in the beautiful temperate winter he returns to the Côte d'Azur where he is professional to the Mont Agel club in Monaco and Mandelieu near Cannes.

Mont Agel is a fascinating place situated on green plateau between the savage mountains of the Alpes Maritimes. It has the most dramatic approach of any course I have ever seen and which for me was emphasised by walking there. A bus, wielded with remarkable skill and timing round impossible corners, takes one from Monaco to La Turbie, which lies on the Grande Corniche, one of Europe's most spectacular roads. The course lies 1,000 ft above La Turbie and is reached by a series of endless hairpin bends which seem to repeat themselves interminably until at last the handsome clubhouse comes into view. One is now 2,500 ft above Monte Carlo and yet seemingly only a full brassie from the shining harbour far below and the white frame of the International Sporting Club where Henry Cotton has his golf school.

The course was made in 1909 and is controlled by the Casino of Monaco. The Prince of that happy little neutrality, which even the Germans failed to abuse seriously, owns to a handicap of sixteen and in all there are some 120 members, of whom one of the best players is the president, J.C. Rey. Although comparatively short, the course can be a formidable test to those who find straightness elusive for the fairways, smooth and green, are bounded by rocks and thick scrub. Two new par five holes are being planned which will increase the length to that of an average British course.

## SHROUDED WORLD SUSPENDED ABOVE THE EARTH

I spent an afternoon there, mostly in the company of Madame Boyer and the president's charming wife, both of whom endured my French with delightful patience, whilst their husbands were occupied, one with teaching and the other with going round in a low score. The day surprisingly was grey and misty and, as the clouds swept low over the mountains, it was as if one was in a secret, shrouded world suspended above the earth with no reminders of human existence. On a normal day the view is magnificent for across the supreme blue of the Mediterranean Corsica's shadow, more than 100 miles away, can be seen.

It was interesting and encouraging to talk with Boyer of the progress of golf in France. When he captained the European side against the American Ryder Cup team at St Cloud in October more than 5,000 spectators paid for admission.

In addition to Mont Agel and Mandelieu there are three other courses on the Riviera – Biot, near Antibes; Mougins near Cannes, and another, Valescure at St Raphael. These provide ready and easily accessible facilities for the huge floating population which invades the coast during the season. But it is not only visitors which sustain golf in this matchless place, because there is a consciousness of the game amongst the French to a far greater extent than before the war.

In numbers France's golfing population is not vast but there is a hard core of enthusiastic players. It should be remembered, too, that golf is not a young game so far as France is concerned and that it was first played at Pau many years ago.

(1953)

# The South American Championship

*Buenos F.H. Ayres*

**TOMORROW MORNING**

The first South American Golf Championship begins here tomorrow, and I have wandered all this distance in order to tell you all about it. The wonderful resources at my command enable me to tell you all about the Championship at this early date, so that you ought to consider yourselves very lucky people to be allowed into the know at a time when other people are still in outer darkness, so to speak, and an astonishingly interesting story it is that I have to tell you, as you yourselves will discover if you read on, which I hope for your own sakes that you will do.

To begin with, you must understand that the golfers here are very keen about their game, and yield to no other players in their enthusiasm. Since I have arrived one man has been shot for doing a hole in one, and the partner in a foursome of a Portuguese Chilean has been seriously injured by a revolver bullet in his spinal column because of his failure to get down a short putt. These little manifestations of keenness are thought little of, however, and go to add to the interest and excitement of the game.

**NEW POT BUNKER**

While practice rounds were in progress the Government of the country changed twice, with little loss of life, the chief damage being the formation of a new pot bunker going to the twelfth, which was cause for regret that at the time of the explosion Don Traversio, the great Mexican player, was addressing his ball on the spot. The ball was lost, and up to the time of writing Don Traversio is also missing. The other entrants, who are thorough sportsmen, greatly regret his disappearance, the more especially because, on the news of the accident reaching the camp, the two British competitors discovered that on account of the midges here and the probability of another rubber boom at home they must needs return at once.

It is very interesting and tremendously profitable to compare the methods of these strenuous South American golfers with those of our own great players and to note the difference, keeping in mind all that tradition means to us and novelty to them, and all that sort of thing, and so on. For example, Pietro Misso, the champion one-eyed player from Uruguay, appears to play with only one club. Having examined this weapon surreptitiously, however, I made the startling discovery that this club is in reality thirteen clubs in one, so our friend Pietro has taken a leaf out of my chum Braid's book, and has disregarded superstitions and at the same time revealed an inherent tendency to traditional ideas, which is rather remarkable, to my way of thinking, and I think a lot between times.

By touching a lever and pressing a button or two Pietro's putter becomes in a trice a driving iron. While examining the club I inadvertently touched a button. Pietro did not seem to notice the change and he attempted to drive off with a putter. When he had examined his club head he shot his caddie, which is a pity, since there are not nearly enough caddies to go round, only the most desperate and adventurous fellows caring to take on the job.

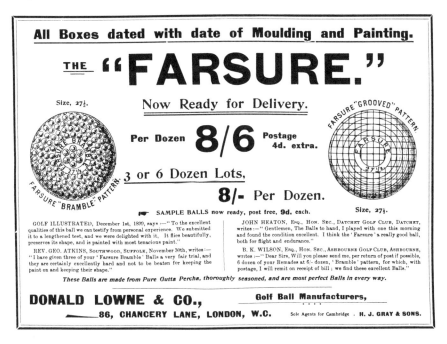

## GOLFER IN A KILT

I have noticed also a striking difference in the way in which these dashing South American players dress themselves for their game. Carramboo, who has come all the way from Honolulu to win fame for the Oahu Country Club, wears a kind of kilt, and a jacket of beads and shells. These players greet each stroke with loud exclamations of delight or disapproval, and they have many pretty ways of describing the particular features of the game.

There is no doubt that they are great golfers, and it will be a very fine thing if some of them should take it into their heads to come over to the Old Country to compete for our own Championship, for it would add to the interest of the meeting and provide no end of sensational incidents in no way connected with golf, so that those of us who think about the game would have no time to weary. I could fill a column and a half quite easily about this alone, but I must get on to the serious part of the Championship, which is what I came out to see and which is what you may or may nor want to read about.

Well, then. Precisely at 9.55 on the morning of the eventful day the first couple strode with gleaming eyes and determined mien and golf clubs on to the first tee. The sun had arisen in all its horrid heat to do its damnedest, and the flies were breakfasting on my ankles. These two were William Brown, of Colorado, a mere stripling of 18 summers, but with the stout heart of a giant, and a nice habit of using his wrists, and Guido Volatile, from Valparaiso, whose beard attracted attention and admiration. I have never seen a great golfer wearing a beard before, except once, at Muirfield, where it is difficult to get a shave. Brown holed a mashie shot for a 5 at the first hole, and the friends of Volatile retired to the clubhouse to make the necessary arrangements for a vendetta. I have the very highest authority for saying that should Brown win his match the Insurance Company intend raising his premiums.

## AN UNLUCKY FIFTEEN

Carramboo's round was somewhat spoilt by a 15 at the seventh. His tee shot landed into a clump of *Mimosa pudica*, and getting out of this he skied the ball among the branches of a prickly pear tree, up which he had to clamber, to his great discomfort. An ant hill caught his sixth, while his seventh struck Guido Volatile in the small of the back. Three more vendettas were entered into upon the spot. I expect to be able to cable some extra spicy stuff tomorrow. The whole of South America is seething with excitement. The cafés here were open all night, and delirious groups were engaged till daybreak disputing the merits of the leading players and discussing their chances of success. Enormous sums have been staked on the result, and one rich guano merchant stands to win two million dollars on Carramboo.

The great Carramboo has just told me that he wouldn't have minded the ant hill had it not been for the ants. He is strongly of the opinion that a local rule ought to have been framed to meet this contingency. I may write about this at some other time. If I don't, you will know that the reason is that other and more weighty matters are occupying my attention.

So here we are at the end of the first day's play in this great Championship, and wonderful things have happened, but are not they all written in the reports of the Press agency whose detailed cable may be found in another column?

(1912)

(1979) "Cacophony? Rubbish! You should consider yourself lucky to have a Supporters Club!"

# The "Unknown" Golf Course in Egypt

*John Knowles, Jun.*

When I say that I am attached to the HBM Wireless Station at Abu Zabal, near Cairo, I betray to a certain extent the whereabouts of what I may aptly describe as an unknown golf course. So, seeing I have gone so far, I may as well say that the course of which I am to write lies about 20 miles north-west of Cairo. Well, as is only to be expected, the soil is of a somewhat sandy nature, and readers will get some idea of what I mean by that when I say that the entire area covers nothing but real North African desert. And not one part of the course extends beyond a space marked off by a dozen 350-foot wireless masts.

As membership is confined solely to the British population at the wireless station, it is, of course, a very limited one. As a matter of fact, we have but 27 members all told, and as several of them are non-players, there is never the slightest fear in the world of any congestion, even at the busiest time of the day! Two couples on the course almost give it the appearance of an Open Championship meeting, but as often as not the place pretty well resembles Aberdeen on a flag day!

Just about a couple of years ago a special endeavour was made to get the house in order. For a start, of course, there were teeing-grounds and "greens" to form, but one great golf architectural difficulty that we did not have to face was that of bunkering. Why, "through the green" could only be likened to one huge bunker! Be that as it may, however, we set about work with a will. For teeing-grounds we could think of nothing better than a few large sized petrol cans, and they proved a very happy choice, too, for they served the purpose admirably. First of all, we got the paint out, and after printing on the number of each hole and the distance we sank them in the sand. But the boxes themselves were not filled with sand. Oh, no! A supply of black Nile mud from a nearby canal solved that little problem. So far so good, we thought, but there was something we had not bargained for.

## FURTHER USES OF A PETROL CAN

In our anxiety to have a course of some kind we had left the wandering Bedouin shepherdesses out of all consideration, so imagine our surprise – perhaps I had better say wrath at our own forgetfulness – when on our arrival at the scene of operations on the following morning we discovered that all our improvised teeing-grounds had gone! It required very little detective work to discover who the robbers were, and that these notoriously clever thieves had come to the conclusion that petrol cans served a much more useful purpose when converted into water-containers.

But we golfers are nothing if not ingenious, and even this dire peril was quickly overcome. We knew full well that if we laid down the second lot of tins just as we had the first we should awake the following morning to see our work once more gone for naught, so before laying them in position we gave them a liberal perforation. And, as we expected, they were once again uprooted by the light of the stars, but this time they were left to lie. Even Bedouins know that perforated cans do not hold water. So one more burial saw that part of the work concluded. This difficulty of the thieves once more confronted us when a little later we decided on a scheme of decoration in which flags and red bunting were to be used. Knowing as I do the propensities of these wanderers of the desert, I straight away calculated that a Bedouin could get along very nicely with a suit made from a few pieces of rag, such as we were supplying absolutely free of charge. But they found no use for sheet tin, so that was that!

Then came the question of the "greens", but this was by no means so difficult a matter as it would seem. In the long run it merely resolved itself into a case of selecting the most level spots, sinking Lyle's Golden Syrup tins, and sticking in the flags. And then a thin top-dressing of well-baked mud supplied quite a tolerably good putting surface. That completed the groundwork, so all that remained now to be done was "playing the course in". Well, that has been proceeded with ever since, and I must say that being able once more to bang hard into the blue gives great satisfaction.

## A LAW UNTO ITSELF

Lastly came the framing of local rules, but these, I am afraid, are very much out of the ordinary run of things, for penalties, while not quite non-existent, are very, very slight. But no one can really appreciate the true reasons for this until one has seen and played over the course. Just to give one or two instances, I may say that sand may be brushed away at each stroke in order to expose no more than three-quarters of the ball, and that a ball may be lifted from any hole made by the foot of a camel, a donkey, or a bare-footed native. But, believe me, for all that one must be playing up to one's very best form and have the good fortune to avoid masts, stays, and so on, to finish all square with Colonel Bogey, who sets the pace at 33. And in conclusion, lest I may have created a mistaken impression as to the standard of Egyptian golf courses, I should just like to say that this course of which I write and over which I play is absolutely a law unto itself. Egypt has many good courses, and I only take a few at random when I mention those at Alexandria and Gezira – both these are well-cared-for grass courses – and the sand courses of Heliopolis and Helouan.

(1927)

**A BALL-SNATCHER'S IMPLEMENT.**

This is a sketch of an instrument used by certain members of the ball-collecting fraternity on the Braid Hills Golf Course. It is simply the handle of a cleek split at the end, with a cork inserted to keep it open. With this the " moucher " can stroll carelessly along the course, and when he comes across a ball the owner of which is probably behind some rising ground he can, without exciting the suspicion of the players in his immediate neighbourhood, pick up the ball and transfer it to his pocket. When walking the split end of the stick is concealed inside the jacket. — *Edinburgh Evening Dispatch.*

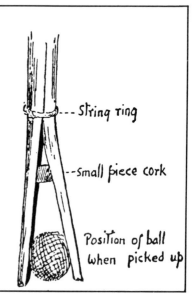

String ring

Small piece cork

Position of ball when picked up

(1899)

# FLIGHTS OF FANTASY

## A Dream of a Match

*Chris Plumridge*

Sitting here in my garret, I am faced with the writer's nightmare: the blank sheet of paper that stares mockingly back at me and, rather like a tricky, downhill putt, the longer I look at it the more problems seem to present themselves. Is it possible, I muse, idly raking over some charred rejection slips in the fireplace, to develop a typewriting twitch? Will there come a day when the fingers will remain arched over the keys, unable to move, until by sheer will-power they are plunged down to tap out a demented tattoo that is the writing equivalent of a four-putt green?

It is hot in the garret. The autumn sun streams through the cracked skylight, inducing a feeling of drowsiness. The mind begins to wander and fantasy takes over. Perhaps it is the sight of the leaves turning on the trees or perhaps it is the scent of damp grass but the visions conjured up are those of a russet Wentworth whose fairways run like green ribbons through an October morning mist. It is World Match-Play time and a sense of anticipation is rife among the crowds that move up the hill towards the first tee. Eight shiny, black limousines are parked in the forecourt, exclusively available for the players during the week. The flags of the nations represented flutter in the light breeze. On the practice ground, eight figures rifle shots away from the dew-laden grass.

Much controversy arose when the dream World Match-Play field was announced. Writing in *The Times*, Bernard Darwin stated that the event could surely not take place without the presence of Harry Vardon, a man, as that revered scribe once wrote, "whose record is so long it must be severely compressed". But the announcement invoked lively comment in the land and the sponsors sat back, secure in the knowledge that the field they had assembled was unlikely to be beaten by any other eight golfers.

The draw was made and panned out thus: Bobby Jones, three times British Open champion, four times winner of the US Open and perpetrator of the Impregnable Quadrilateral in 1930 was drawn to play Samuel Jackson Snead, three times US Masters winner, three times US PGA winner and 1946 British Open champion. In the second match, Ben Hogan, winner of all golf's major titles and four times US Open champion is to play Gary Player, five times World Match-Play winner and also winner of all golf's major titles. Match number three brought together Walter Hagen, whose four consecutive US PGA titles between the years 1924-27 marks him as the supreme match player, and Arnold Palmer, twice winner of the World Match-Play, twice winner of the British Open, four times winner of the US Masters and 1960 US Open champion. In the final match, Jack Nicklaus, the man with more major titles to his name than anyone is due to face Henry Cotton, thrice British Open champion and the man responsible for the elevated status now enjoyed by British professionals.

The starter's voice boomed out, "Match number one, on the tee Mr Robert T Jones." The familiar plus-fours-clad figure strode forward and with that lovely, long, languid swing sent the ball sailing down the fairway to the crest of the hill. On his heels came Snead, the straw hat set at a jaunty angle. His drive flew long, but tailed away at the end and left him an awkward shot from the right across a sea of scrub. A large crowd followed the match as it progressed out into the country, but many stayed to witness the arrival of Hogan and Player. Hogan stepped forward on to the tee, coiled and cracked the ball arrow-straight. His face betrayed not an iota of emotion and Player, perhaps remembering the awe in which he held his opponent, rather hurried his tee shot and hooked it into the left-hand rough.

## STROKE AFTER STROKE OF PERFECT WEIGHT

A burst of laughter greeted the next combatant – Hagen, acting out his philosophy of always stopping to smell the flowers by kissing a pretty girl and admiring the rose tucked in her buttonhole. Hagen was dressed in black-and-white brogue shoes, Argyll socks, cream plus-fours and a yellow sweater.

With barely a glance down the fairway, he lunged at the ball and sent it swinging away into the right-hand rough. Turning to the crowd, he said: "That stuff I was on last night didn't make me drunk, but I sure as hell fell down a lot." Even Palmer joined in the laughter for that one before he set down to the business of driving his tee shot far down the fairway, arms high in that familiar finishing flourish.

And finally the last two, Cotton and Nicklaus. Cotton looked taut, his face drawn, the shoulders sloped in the revealing left-to-right plane. He teed up and the hands moved through the shot and the ball fizzed from the tee as the striker reached that characteristic braced left-leg finishing position. Up stepped Nicklaus. With a massive wind-up he crashed the ball so far that it came to rest on the downslope of that first fairway, leaving its owner a nasty shot from an awkward stance.

Fortunes fluctuated wildly that first morning. Jones lunched abstemiously on a glass of milk and a sandwich, knowing that his one-hole lead over Snead would mean a supreme effort in the afternoon. Hogan stood five up on Player after 18 as the American had staged a near-repeat of his 1956 Canada Cup appearance on the same course and had played the first 10 holes in 35 strokes. Player, suffering from a vicious hook, repaired immediately to the practice ground. Hagen lunched on three Scotches to partner the three-hole deficit he was carrying against Palmer. Nicklaus and Cotton were all square, both having gone round in 68.

As the afternoon drew on it quickly became plain that Snead would not catch Jones as the amateur produced stroke after stroke of perfect weight

"ONE CROWDED HOUR OF GLORIOUS LIFE

—IS WORTH AN AGE WITHOUT A NAME."

(1901)                    THE GOLFER'S REVERIE.

and direction and when the match finished on the 15th green, Jones needed three fours for a 67. Player, meanwhile was staging one of his renowned fight-backs and turned in 32 to wrest three of the five holes back. An eagle at the 12th by the South African put him only one down, but an imperious 3-iron by Hogan round the edge of the trees on the 15th gave the American a birdie putt which he holed to go back to two up.

They halved the 16th, and on the famous 17th Hogan struck two woods that sent the ball arching towards the green and Player's putt for a birdie slid by leaving him the vanquished and Hogan the victor.

Hagen, by dint of some remarkable recoveries, was still only two down as he and Palmer played the 13th and it was here that Hagen played the shot that was to break Palmer's heart. Cutting his second away to the right off that elusive green, Hagen found his ball buried in a clump of tall grass with a bunker between him and a pin that was set close to the right-hand side of the green. Forsaking all the usual preliminaries, Hagen thumped the ball out and it ran round the edge of the bunker, finally resting a few inches from the hole. A stunned Palmer three-putted to lose that hole. Another three putts at the next from the lower level and a hooked drive on 16 put him one down and, with Hagen making a wondrous four on the last from under the trees to the right of the green, Palmer was closed out by two holes.

The Nicklaus-Cotton saga saw the finest golf of that first day and both men came to the last all square. Two massive blows by the American saw him home in two and when his putt from fully 15 yards plunged into the hole. Cotton could only manage a wry grin as he walked forward to shake hands.

So the semi-finals were set between Jones and Hogan, artistry versus ice-cool precision, and Hagen versus Nicklaus, showmanship versus power. O.B. Keeler, Jones's close friend and reporter on all his man's great triumphs, felt that the Atlantan would be hard-pressed to sustain his energies for another 36 holes of gruelling combat. Hogan, on the other hand, was wrapped in that cocoon of concentration that had so impressed the Scots at Carnoustie 1953.

Jones swept away in the morning round striking woods smack into the heart of the greens and wielding Calamity Jane to deadly effect. Hogan's Achilles Heel, the short putt, proving his undoing on at least three holes and the man from Texas went into lunch four down. A tiring Jones was hauled back to only two up with three to play but a silky putt wafted across the 16th green and dropped to give the amateur a 3 and 2 win.

The other semi-final was really no contest. Hagen, who had booked a passage home on the QE2, seemed to have his mind fixed on the delights of life afloat and only some staunch recoveries kept the margin below the 12 and 11 defeat that Nicklaus inflicted upon him.

And so to a final that brought together the greatest of two eras if one used the criteria of major championships. Was there ever a match like it? A morning 66 by Nicklaus left him only one up as Jones produced a 67, the 17th, which Nicklaus eagled, being the only difference between them. The afternoon saw a freshening wind swirling through the trees and Jones, drawing on some hidden reserves of strength, flighted his shots low and true while Nicklaus watched some of his high-flying approaches catch the wind and swing away. Nicklaus putted phenomenally and was one down at the turn. They halved the next five, two of them with birdies and stepped on to the 15th tee. Here Nicklaus unleashed a colossal drive that left him only a 4-iron into the green. When the shot squirmed to a halt only three feet from the hole, the match was all square. The 16th was halved in 4s, the 17th in cagey 5s and with the crowd almost beside itself, they marched to the last tee.

## ORCHESTRATED BY AN UNSEEN CONDUCTOR

Jones's drive was long, low and possessed of that hint of fade that took it to the corner of the dog-leg. Nicklaus's drive was also long and also faded, but it was a fraction too high and the wind pushed it back so it came to rest twenty yards behind his opponent's. In a manner reminiscent of his drive to the 18th at St Andrews during the last round of the 1970 Open, Nicklaus took off his sweater and, drawing back his 3-wood, hit a stroke of such calculated power that those who saw it swear the ball gave an agonised cry. It was a stroke of sheer majesty and no one was surprised when the ball came to rest only 20 feet from the pin. How would Jones react? The answer was not long in coming. Jones too swung a 3-wood and the shot set of for the target as if held on line by an invisible hand, it pitched short of the green, skirted the bunker and ran up to lie twelve feet from the hole. It was an ecstatic moment as the two players walked through the cheering throng and then, as if orchestrated by an unseen conductor, the crowd fell silent as Nicklaus weighed up his putt. After what seemed an age, he struck it and the collective gasp from the spectators meant that it had just edged by. Now it was Jones's turn. He crouched behind his putt, brow furrowed in concentration, he stepped up and the soft sound Calamity Jane made

signalled the start of the ball on its path, the ball curled down the gentle slope and . . .

It was now cold in the garret. The sun had long set but through the murky shadows I could still see the blank sheet of paper staring back at me, defying me to mark its surface. The dream World Match-Play was over but I felt that somewhere in the recess of my mind lurked the germ of an idea. With eager fingers I began to type.

(1979)

## "Lines Penned by a Golfer Under Nicotine Drug Withdrawal Fantasies"

_Peter Dobereiner_

Morning, men. Nice day we've got for it. No thanks, old chap, I've given up. Funny thing, I never noticed before that you can really _smell_ spring in the air. Just one of the bonuses of packing up fags, I suppose. You know, for years I fancied I had sinus trouble and I was actually thinking about nipping round to the quack to see if they ought to be syringed, or whatever they do with sinuses. But since kicking the filthy habit the old nasal passages have been as clear as the streets of Tel Aviv on a flag day. What? No, cut it out clean. Haven't touched one since Thursday.

Now, how are we going to split up? No offence, Roy, but if it's all the same I'd rather not play with you today. Delightful chap and all that but I think I'd better keep among non-smokers for a bit. Out of smell, out of mind and all that. Keep right away from temptation and keep active – that's the secret of giving up smoking. Right, let's get going – me and Phil will take on Bob and Eric, ball a corner and no holds barred. Are we on? Good. Excellent. Fine. Let's have at it, then. What? Just a quick half? How long is that going to take, for God's sake? One half and then another. Dammit we'll be in here all afternoon before you know where we are. What is this, anyway – a golf club or a damn boozing society? All right. All right! ALL RIGHT! I'm sorry. Certainly, a quick half would be nice. Thank you.

_Now_ can we make a start? Hey! What the hell's Eric up to? He's getting in another round! No. I haven't joined the temperance league but it is just that when you first come off fags the old craving is strongest when you are sitting round having a quiet drink. That's when you really feel it and you get a bit irritable and fidgety. Oh, sorry Bob. Steward! Chuck us a cloth, will you? There, that will hardly show if you keep your sweater pulled well down. Of course a bit of beer won't make it shrink.

Well, I am going to get my shoes on. See you lads on the first tee.

### WHERE HAVE YOU BEEN?

Where have you been? I've been kicking my heels for half an hour. What? No, of course I didn't nip away to get out of my round. It's just that I can't stand wasting the whole day in a smoky bar. All right. It's my shout when we get in. Now can we please get on with it. For Pete's sake! We can work out the shots as we walk up the first. Will somebody, anybody, whack off. Here, let the dog see the rabbit.

Damn! Sorry, Phil. I'm afraid I'll have to leave this hole to you. Bit quick on the old backswing. Never mind. I'll hit another just to keep you company after old Bob's finished dithering about there on the tee.

Yes, Phil. I do appreciate that we are four down after four holes. I am also only too painfully aware that my swing is slightly on the quick side. That much is blatantly obvious without any patronising advice from a 22-handicapper, thank you very much. Don't worry; it will come good in time. That was a pretty crisp iron I hit into the short hole. So? What's so strange about five-putting? It could happen to anybody on these damn greens. That oaf of a greenkeeper ought to be shot. I can't think why the club employs such a feeble-minded twit. At least, I *can* think why – the whole greens committee is composed of feeble-minded twits. Jack Nicklaus himself couldn't get his ball near the hole on that third green. Bob? That was sheer fluke. You know I never noticed it before but Bob has got some pretty unpleasant habits on the golf course. The way he waggles his club before he hits the ball. Absurd, I call it. Nothing but time wasting. I suspect he only does it because he knows we all like to play quickly.

Here we go again. Look, can we invoke the five-minute rule while Eric hunts for his blasted tee peg? I think you are doing it on purpose just to get us impatient and edgy. Well, it won't work. You can't upset my unruffled calm with that kind of snide gamesmanship. Oh for God's sake get out of the way, man! Right, I'm going to pretend my ball is Eric and sock it half a mile up the fairway . . . BLAST! I honestly wouldn't have thought it possible to go out of bounds on that side.

All right, Phil. I've said I'm sorry. Bob shouldn't have been standing behind me when I was taking a few practice swings. It's only a bit of a graze.

That limp is sheer affectation to get us rattled. Well, it doesn't fool me. And if he offers once more to run into the club and get me a packet of cigarettes, I'll crack him on the other ankle. I keep telling you all that it doesn't bother me not having a cigarette. I'm perfectly all right so long as we don't dawdle about.

**"THEY'RE FOR GOLF, CUT THE BOTTOMS OF THE POCKETS WILL YOU?"**

### I ONLY SMOKE FILTERS

Just look at the mess on this tee. Why they can't pick up all the debris when they empty the waste baskets beats me. Get a load of the size of that dog-end. There must be four or five really good drags left in it. You think you've got some matches in the glove pocket? Don't be revolting. Do you honestly imagine I would stoop to stooping down to pick up somebody's dog-end? Anyway, I only smoke filters. That is I only _used_ to smoke filters.

You know, Phil, you aren't making much of a game of it for us. That's the match and the bye. Do you think I'm made of golf balls? I can't imagine what persuaded the handicapping committee to cut you to 22. Granted I am having a bit of an off-day but that can happen to anybody. The way you hoik at the ball you have no chance.

Lord! Don't use that tone of voice with me, you sanctimonious prig. A socket can happen to anybody at any time and he ought to have realised it. Walking along like that while I was playing the shot. And I did shout Fore. The doddering old fool should have ducked. Eric? Eric? Loosen his collar a bit. No I don't think it's serious; his lips always are a bit blueish. Eric? Stop mucking about. Turn him over on his back. There! I thought he'd be all right again in a jiffy. We'll get some ice from the steward when we get in to take down the swelling. Sorry about that, Eric old man, but you shouldn't really have been over there.

Right, this to save the bye-bye. What do you think Phil? A touch of left lip? I'll roll her straight into the back of the cup. Now look here, you two. You've been pulling these diabolical strokes all the way round. You've won the match and the bye. Do you think I could have just one putt without you rattling your blasted clubs about like castanets? Perhaps you'd like to come over and stamp my ball into the turf as well. No, I'm not narked because we're losing; it is just that for one single putt I'd like the game to be played in the gentlemanly spirit of consideration for one's opponent.

Now look what you've made me do. Chuck us my sand iron, will you Phil. I might just sink it. Oh, no chance! Look at that lie! Some blasted pigeon has been trampling through the bunker and I'm right in a heel mark. All right, ornithological genius, pigeons don't have heels. Claw marks, then!

No, we won't bother looking for it. Let the ball rot in the bushes for ever for all I care. Look, if you don't mind I won't hang about for a drink. Another time. I'll nip straight off. Pay my debts for me, will you Phil, and I'll settle with you later. I've only got three 10p pieces and I'll need them for the machine . . .

Funny thing about those three. They're no fun to play with any more. (1974)

## Fora! Fora! Fora!

*Chris Plumridge*

They came in low and fast that morning with the sun hard at their backs. Their track marks in the dew were the only indication of their arrival and before the secretary had even unlocked the door to his office, they were in possession of the first tee, the pro's shop and the locker-room.

## A GOLF PIPE.

This is the latest novelty which has been brought out for the benefit of the golfing community. The wonder is that the thing has not been attempted before, seeing how readily the implements of the game lend themselves to miniature reproduction, not only in jewellery but in other forms of ornamental and decorative art. The Golf Pipe is elegant in appearance and practical in use, as it can be smoked with or without the long stem, and the Golfer who indulges in the fragrant weed will be able to enjoy a long pipe while reading, or a short one at cards or billiards. The stem of the pipe is an exact reproduction of the club, but of course, proportionately smaller, and the bowl, which is made of briar or meerschaum, resembles a Golf ball, both in size and appearance.

The pipe can be obtained through any tobacconist from the makers of the well-known brand of Pipes. Judging from the specimen now before us, the makers seem to have produced this interesting novelty in material of excellent quality and high finish of workmanship. We cannot imagine a more suitable prize for competition than the long Golf Pipe with meerschaum bowl, and handsome case covered with Russia leather. The short briar pipe will be found a useful addition to the Golfer's outfit.

(1892)

Lifting his binoculars to his one good eye, he'd lost the other at West Hill, the secretary saw that the task was almost beyond him. They'd moved too quickly and suddenly for him to mount anything but a futile gesture. Dragging his gammy leg, the result of a severed tendon from an earlier skirmish, he called over Nigger, his faithful black labrador and limped to lock the door to the ladies' locker-room. He knew it was a meaningless action at this stage but he was damned if he was going to let them completely overrun the club without showing some kind of spirit.

"Well, Nig, old boy," he said to the animal that looked up at him with large brown eyes, tail wagging furiously, "it looks like the end of the road for you and me but as long as there are men proud to call themselves British, as along as there's a flag to salute, then it's worth going on even if it means making the ultimate sacrifice." And the secretary stumped off to meet the commander of the invasion force.

The Captain of the Micro-Widget Manufacturing Company Golfing Society was an honourable man. Educated at Oxford, he admired the British but felt them to be soft and in need of discipline. When the secretary entered the men's locker-room the Captain of the MWMCGS bowed deep and low. "Blitish secletaly," he said, baring his teeth in an apology for a smile, "Blitish secletaly will be preased to hand orer keys to erectric caddie cart shed." The enormity of this request was like a body blow to the secretary but his face betrayed none of his emotions. "I am afraid," replied the secretary, "that I cannot accede to your request."

"In rat case," said the Japanese captain, "you reave me with no artelnative but to ret my men roose on your course. Prease to step outside where my men will show Impelial Japanese golfers do not take kindry to instluctions from Blitish pig dog secletaly."

Outside was already a shambles – the greens staff had been horded into the gang mower shed, their engines silenced. The pro lay gibbering in the corner of his shop as one of the invaders read him the complete volumes of Isao Aoki's 'Guide to the Oriental golf swing', the sing-song tones acting as a refined form of water torture.

The steward had been forced into the kitchen where he had been ordered to prepare 50 meals comprising fresh bamboo shoots, long grain rice and chicken in soya sauce with saki to follow. The door to the electric caddie cart shed had been broken down and a squadron of carts, the Rising Sun flag fluttering from their bonnets, were patrolling the area round the first tee.

## HE CAME AT THEM HEAD ON

It was "Sailor" who was first to arrive. "Sailor", a veteran of Wentworth and the Old Course, a man who knew electric caddie cart strategy better than anyone. They still talked about him in the mess and how, in one dog-fight, piloting a Hurricane type cart with only two wheels and half his golf clubs gone, he'd seen off six of the enemy. All they'd found of him afterwards was a leg and a piece of offal in the tee-peg compartment but Sir Archie had done a wonderful job of stitching him up and he was soon back in action.

This time he came at them head on, there was no time for cover or a subtle approach, he knew he had to hit and run and wear them down with the ferocity of his attack. Bearing down from the car park, and being a stickler for discipline, taking care to avoid the white lines indicating the area for the President's Rolls, he burst through the phalanx of Rising Sun flags. With a thrust of his new graphite-shafted brassie he took three of the enemy out on his first run, wheeled, and swiftly changing to a sand-wedge, removed two more on the return.

Confusion reigned in the Japanese ranks – they scattered, many of them belching flame from their engines, careering on a disaster course to plunge into the abyss that was the cross-bunker on the first fairway. Before they had time to re-group, "Sailor" was back, spitting defiance from his 1-iron with the grooved hosel and offset leading edge.

It was over almost as soon as it had begun. The tattered remnants of the MWMCGS, once a proud and arrogant body of men each committed to the five hour round and the keeping of every score, limped back to the clubhouse while the secretary ran up the Union Jack on the club flag-pole. "I am prepared," said the secretary, "to accept the unconditional surrender of your forces under the terms empowered to me by the Royal & Ancient Convention." The Japanese captain once again bowed deep and low: "Prease," he said, "to accept folmal sullender but understand that for Japanese is no honour in defeat, onry shame." With that he drew his ceremonial putter and fell forwards onto the sharp end, uttering scarcely a moan as his blood tainted the velvet sward of the putting-green.

"Strange fellows," said the secretary, looking down at his faithful black labrador and tapping his gammy leg with his wooden cane, "they used to do that when we saw them off the Burma Road."

(1986)

## Impressions of the Open Championship of 2027

*G.A. Philpot*

The First Day's Play

**June 24th** Remarkable golf was witnessed today at the 5th National Course when the opening rounds of the British Open Championship were decided. The original entry, it will be remembered, consisted of 7,200 players, every nation being well represented. Prominent among those who had survived the qualifying rounds were Chung Foo Wang and Brilliant Fling, the Chinese champion and ex-champion; Abraham Isaacs, the Palestine wonder; Paul Wagga Wagga, the Solomon Islands' crack; Michaelovitch Szywpkcwopski and Evan Zkpfmatzbdzapoff, the Russian experts; Herr Blitzen and Herr von Eider der Uder, of Berlin; and Babe Booth, Red Sox, Battling Firearms, Derk X. Yonkerman, Nick Y. Zoomph and Gene Q. Vaddy, the American stars, who between them have won twenty-four national championships. Of the remaining qualifiers, the representatives of England included Percy Smith, James Brown and George Robinson, the very popular professionals; while Hector Macduff, Brian Neill and Ian Stewart represented Scotland, and Murphy O'Shaughnessy, Ireland.

The course was in splendid condition, the greens being in particularly fine order, thanks to the newly invented Dio-peroxide grass-growing rays, which had been applied overnight by Professor Scroggins, F.G.G.S., the world-famed greenkeeper. The professor, who gets a salary of £7,000 a year, rightly considers his invention is going to revolutionise grass culture, for he can now make grass grow where none grew before. It is understood that a syndicate has been formed with the object of applying the new invention to the problem of premature baldness in centenarians.

The actual length of the course, as played from the championship teeing-grounds, is 12,351 yards. To our obscure forefathers of a century ago, such a distance might have appeared long, but nowadays, with a ball which easily travels a matter of 600 yards off the wooden clubs, the course is really on the short side; and, in my opinion, the time has come when the authorities must consider seriously the question of standardisation ball, so as to preserve a reasonable ratio between the length of the holes and the distance which can be obtained by the ball.

**DISASTER ON SPECTATORS' OVERHEAD RAILWAY**
Another problem which will have to be tackled shortly is the crowd. A few decades ago, when only seventy or eighty thousand spectators witnessed the play, they could be controlled very easily. But today, when 200,000 people were present, the defects of the present system were only too obvious. For example, an accident, as disgraceful as it was disastrous, occurred this morning on the Spectators' Overhead Never-Stop Railway near the 9th green, when Red Sox was holing-out a chip of 160 yards to reach the turn in 29.

In his anxiety to see the result of the shot, a gentleman wearing horn-rimmed glasses and a big black cigar pushed the driver overboard, and the car, bounding forward violently, collided with another vehicle in front, with appalling results for all concerned. Both cars were derailed and fell into the Z114 bunker by the 9th green, just as a Lapland competitor, who was trapped therein, was addressing the ball. Ultimately, when the wrecked vehicles were removed, no trace of the unlucky North Pole champion could be found, and the Control Board were appealed to by the marker as to the correct ruling in the case of a lost player. Up to the moment of writing no decision has been arrived at, but meanwhile the competitor's right boot has been found among the debris.

Mention, too, must be made of the ungentlemanly conduct of the crowd assembled in the grandstand by the 6th green. It seems that Percy Smith, the Melton Mowbray professional, and a British hope, had a shot of 300 yards for his second and, over-clubbing himself by taking an iron where a mashie would have been ample, his ball pitched into the middle of the occupants of the two-guinea seats, doing considerable damage to an old gentleman's thyroid gland. Certain hostile members of the crowd, apparently of Surrey extraction, rushed upon the course, and seized Smith's clubs, whereupon another portion of the grand-stand, obviously sympath-isers from Leicestershire, joined in the *mêlée*. Eventually the flying squad of the National Course Special Police arrived by aeroplane from the club-house, and by directing invisible rays upon the combatants, paralysed their nervous systems and peace was restored. Smith was ordered by the referee to carry on by dropping another ball not nearer the grandstand under penalty of one stroke, but the Englishman wilted visibly under the strain and ultimately took 10 to the hole.

Not for 75 years has a British representative won the championship and it does not look as if this particular "record" will be disturbed on the present occasion, for at the end of today's play Red Sox, the famous Cincinatti fire-eater, leads the field with a score of 117 for the 36 holes, followed by Nick Y. Zoomph, the Boston course-burner, with 120. Two strokes further behind are Szywpkcwopski and Zkpfmatzbdzapoff, the mighty Moscow smiters. Curiously enough, these two famous golfing artists are cousins, both wear beards which they tuck in under their woollies when playing, and both train on pickled boar and iced vodka.

Of the British representatives Percy Smith did best. He finished six strokes behind the leader, and but for the unfortunate episode at the 6th, particulars of which have already been related, he would be in a much better position. Murphy O'Shaughnessy, the sole Irish survivor of the

(1892)                                                    Ginger Beer Hole St. Andrews,

qualifying rounds, was disqualified early this morning for playing with an explosive ball. The discovery was made on the 4th green by the marker, who by chance picked the ball up after O'Shaughnessy had holed out, and discovered that it was not only nearly red-hot, but that sulphurous fumes were emanating from it.

Of Red Sox's play no praise could be too high. Whether it was due to the electronised ball he was using, or whether to the copious quantities of peptonised chewing-gum which he consumed on the way round I cannot say, but the fact remains that he played some great golf. At the long 8th, for example, he reached the green, 1375 yards away, with two full shots and holed a putt of over 19 yards for a useful 3. At the short 10th (493 yards) he played a mashie shot to the green with so much back-spin that a shower of sparks emanated from the head of the club as it established contact with the ball. But the real strength of his golf lay in his game round and on the greens. On no single occasion from 50 yards and under did he fail to hole out in one stroke. This was a standard just a shade better than his rivals, and a repetition of it tomorrow must bring success to the genial Cincinatti giant.

By the way, the American contingent – Yonkerman, Booth, Firearms, Sox, Zoomph and Vaddy – flew back to New York at the conclusion of the day's play for a Turkish bath. They will, however, leave tomorrow morning at 6.30 am by the Special Transatlantic Aerial Express, and will therefore be back at the 5th National Course in good time for breakfast. Their trainer, Ruddy Goode, accompanied the party.

(1927)

## The Lighter Side

_Wanda Morgan_

The ability to miss the ball is considered the prerogative of the veriest "rabbit", and yet there must be many instances of first-class golfers emulating a feat that usually calls for jeers and not cheers. I know all about the historic instance of Harry Vardon missing the ball on the green during the progress of the American Open Championship in 1900 at Wheaton, Illinois, which, incidentally, he won. It will be recalled by those who saw it, and those who have read about it, that in attempting to knock a putt of a few inches into the hole with one hand he struck the ground with his club and never touched the ball at all. But I am not referring to incidents that may be said to have resulted through sheer carelessness. I mean a really honest attempt to hit the ball that proved unsuccessful.

I only know of one, and that a somewhat unique effort. It occurred on the first tee of the old course at Addington, and the player was a Scottish International. The ground was frozen hard. With his first attempt the club-head touched a lump of ground behind the ball which threw it up and over the top of the ball. The chagrin of the player was only equalled by the unrestrained mirth of the onlookers. However, he pulled himself together, and showed the dourness of his origin by the determined manner in which he proceeded to address himself to the second attempt. And he showed his quality as a golfer by the accuracy with which he struck the ball at this second attempt, FOR IT WENT INTO THE HOLE.

That is a perfectly true story, and it is the most fantastic one I know of missing the ball, and then doing a hole in one which could not be counted as a hole in one.

Of course, of humorous misses, the one recorded in *The Golfer's Handbook* always strikes me as wanting a lot of beating. It relates to a Mayor in an English Midland town in declaring a course open being asked to putt on the home green. "Whether the 'crowd' unnerved him or his eye was out," says *The Golfer's Handbook*, "is not known, but the Mayor missed the ball completely!" The pomp and ceremony attaching to that instance I can well imagine, and the thought of such a *contretemps* at such a moment makes an appeal to my risibility that is always beyond my control.

## CAPT. ASTON NAILS THE OPPOSITION

Another episode, though it cannot be strictly included among the missing the ball items, which always starts me off laughing is connected with Capt. Gordon Aston, an inveterate joker on the golf links. On this occasion Capt. Aston conceived the idea of driving a nine-inch nail through a golf ball, sawing off its head and filling in the space with gutta-percha and paint. So the ball looked perfectly all right except on one side; on that side, of course protruded a goodly portion of the nail.

Thus armed, Capt. Aston awaited his opportunity in a four-ball match in which he was engaged. This opportunity occurred when his own ball and the ball of one of his opponents came to rest on a green in close proximity to each other. Hurrying on, he reached the balls well ahead of the unsuspecting opponent, and, bending over the latter's, shouted out: "May I see if this is mine?" The answer being in the affirmative, he proceeded to substitute the ball with the nail for the good one, taking care to push the nail right into the ground.

The opponent took great pains (as he always did) to find the correct line; addressed his ball and swung his putter at it with his usual deliberation; the putter met the ball, but the ball did not move! To say that the striker received a shock would be to put it mildly. He was clearly dumbfounded, as so were two of the remaining three players and their caddies. But Capt. Aston had to burst out laughing at the complete astonishment that was being registered all round, and the game was up!

Something similar to this was once worked, so it is related, on that great and venerable St Andrews figure, Thomas Linskill. When Linskill came out to play his afternoon foursome after a very excellent lunch, a heavily bribed caddie teed-up a ball that had painted on it concentric circles of many hues. As soon as he got a proper sight of this amazing ball on the tee, Linskill obviously began to wonder if all was well with him. He shut his eyes and then opened them again; he shook his head and once more focused this strange object to find that it retained its strangeness. That settled it. Verily he was ill unto death. And without speaking one word he walked away from the tee, up the big steps and into the clubhouse!

(1933)

. . . and finally a punishment to fit the crime!

## Boy Hanged for Stealing Golf Balls

In an interesting note on "Golf in Banff in Early Times" published in the *Banffshire Journal* a writer says: "The earliest reference to Golf in the records of the burgh of Banff is in the year 1637, when Francis Brown, 'ane boy of ane evill lyiff,' was hanged on the Gallows Hill of Banff for, *inter alia*, stealing 'some Golff ballis,' two of which he confessed 'he sauld to Thomas Urquhartis servand.' The numerous references to club makers in the burgh records leave little if any doubt that Golf has, at least since the above date, been played continuously on the Links of Banff. In Banff Museum is a skull, labelled that of Macpherson, the noted freebooter. The skull was found prior to a recent complete examination of the burgh records, and when the belief was entertained that Macpherson alone suffered death on the Gallows Hill. The evidence points, however, more strongly towards the skull being that of this infamous Golf-ball stealer, and I would respectfully suggest to the Museum Committee that the skull be re-labelled as that of the aforesaid Francis Brown, in order to point a moral and serve as a warning to all future generations of the danger and disgrace of stealing Golf balls."

(1891)